MW00576118

The SHEPHERD
AS
THEOLOGIAN

John MacArthur
GENERAL EDITOR

HARVEST HOUSE PUBLISHERS
EUGENE, OREGON

Unless otherwise indicated, all Scripture quotations are from the New American Standard Bible®, © 1960, 1962, 1963, 1968, 1971, 1972, 1973, 1975, 1977, 1995 by The Lockman Foundation. Used by permission. (www.Lockman.org)

Verses marked NKJV are taken from the New King James Version®. Copyright © 1982 by Thomas Nelson, Inc. Used by permission. All rights reserved.

Cover by Harvest House Publishers

Cover Image © Greg Rakozy / Unsplash

THE SHEPHERD AS THEOLOGIAN

Copyright © 2017 by Grace Community Church
Published by Harvest House Publishers
Eugene, Oregon 97402
www.harvesthousepublishers.com

ISBN 978-0-7369-6211-7 (pbk.)
ISBN 978-0-7369-6212-4 (eBook)

Library of Congress Cataloging-in-Publication Data
Names: MacArthur, John, 1939- editor.
Title: The shepherd as theologian / John MacArthur, general editor.
Description: Eugene, Oregon : Harvest House Publishers, 2017. | Includes
    bibliographical references.
Identifiers: LCCN 2016046227 (print) | LCCN 2016047434 (ebook) | ISBN
    9780736962117 (hardcover) | ISBN 9780736962124 (ebook)
Subjects: LCSH: Theology, Doctrinal. | Calvinism. | Reformed
    Church—Doctrines.
Classification: LCC BT80 .S47 2017 (print) | LCC BT80 (ebook) | DDC
    230/.42—dc23
LC record available at https://lccn.loc.gov/2016046227

All rights reserved. No part of this publication may be reproduced, stored in a retrieval system, or transmitted in any form or by any means—electronic, mechanical, digital, photocopy, recording, or any other—except for brief quotations in printed reviews, without the prior permission of the publisher.

Printed in the United States of America

17 18 19 20 21 22 23 24 25 / ML-GL / 10 9 8 7 6 5 4 3 2 1

CONTENTS

INTRODUCTION

For nearly four decades, the Shepherds' Conference has been committed to what the Reformers began 500 years ago.

The essence of the Reformation was to rescue the Word from the shackles of Roman Catholic tyranny, corruption, and heresy. The Reformers knew the significance of getting back to the Word, as John Calvin wrote: "Christ reigns whenever He subdues the world to Himself by the preaching of His Word." That is why the goal of the Shepherds' Conference has always been to live out Paul's mandate to Timothy: "The things which you have heard from me in the presence of many witnesses, entrust these to faithful men who will be able to teach others also" (2 Timothy 2:2).

At the Shepherds' Conference we've had the unique privilege to participate in encouraging and equipping men to declare the truth. What started as a small gathering of 159 individuals has, by God's grace, blossomed into an international movement with thousands in attendance each spring. Over the years, pastors from every state and nearly 100 countries have come to the conference to be challenged and encouraged in the areas of preaching, theology, leadership, discipleship, and counseling.

Since its inception, the Shepherds' Conference has featured hundreds of sermons specifically directed at pastors and church leaders. Because the truth of God's Word is timeless, those messages are still as rich and powerful today as when they were first preached. That is why I was so grateful when Harvest House Publishers approached me about publishing this third volume—a collection of the most memorable Shepherds' Conference messages on various theological topics.

A fundamental quality that set the Reformers apart from today's modern pastors is that they were theologians and biblical scholars. However, for a couple of centuries now, pastors have outsourced doctrine to the academy. The pastor must once again become the theologian, biblical scholar, and guardian of sound doctrine.

My desire has been for the Shepherds' Conference to participate in the multiplication of pastor-theologians. May this book help all spiritual leaders, whether you've been to the Shepherds' Conference or not, think deeply about the things of God. As you read it, my prayer is that your passion for truth will burn brighter and your resolve for Christ's glory will grow stronger as you seek to serve and lead His church.

For the Great Shepherd,

John MacArthur

THE LORD'S GREATEST PRAYER, PART 1

"Holy Father, keep them in Your name,
the name which You have given Me."

JOHN 17:11

1

THE LORD'S GREATEST PRAYER, PART 1

John MacArthur

Shepherds' Conference 2016

John 17

No profession in the world suffers from a more serious lack of clarity, when it comes to the basic requirements of the job, as the pastorate. Everyone but pastors seems to know what their job is. In fact, if we are honest, clergy malpractice goes on everywhere, all the time. It is ubiquitous. It is pandemic. There is widespread confusion about what it means to be a pastor, and widespread indifference to prescribed biblical duties. As a result, the church has no concept of what the pastor is to be or do.

Where Is the Pastor-Theologian?

One thing is clear: Most pastors have no interest in being theologians, nor do their congregations expect them to be. The devolution of theology and biblical scholarship as a serious matter for Christians can be traced back to the absence of doctrine and careful biblical scholarship in the pulpit. This is a dereliction of duty. This is clergy malpractice. The pastorate is no longer an intellectual calling, and no longer do pastors provide serious intellectual leadership. Today's pastors do not move in the realm of theology; instead, they manage programs. They give uplifting talks, apply culturally invented principles, and pour their energy into everything but scholarship—everything but an intense study of the text, which yields sound doctrine.

They are practitioners rather than theologians. At best, today's pastors broker other people's ideas, which are selected carefully by their own whims and desires and the popularity of certain people. Pastors have become middle managers who broker other people's theology and other people's ideas. Whatever happened to speaking the things fitting for sound doctrine? For the goal of biblical exposition is doctrine first—to draw out of the text the doctrine, the truth—and then to show its implications, application, and exhortation. Above all other things, the pastor is to teach doctrine.

Not only that, but the pastor is also the guardian of sound doctrine. He is to protect the theological integrity of divine truth before his people, in his place, and in his generation. For a couple of centuries now, pastors have outsourced doctrine to the academy.

If you were to go back to the nineteenth century, the majority of university presidents in the United States were ordained pastors. Things have changed since then. In 1977 (after I had been at Grace Community Church for about 8 years), I received a phone call from James Montgomery Boice, and he asked me if I would come and serve on the International Council on Biblical Inerrancy that produced the Chicago Statement on Biblical Inerrancy. I was shocked. I was just a local pastor here at Grace Community Church, I was in my thirties, and I was out of my league. When I got to the first meeting in Chicago, I was stunned by the fact that there were only 2 pastors—myself and Jim Boice. The other 98 men came from academic institutions. And the fact that they picked me says something about how difficult it was to find somebody else to go with Boice! While there I sat in conversations with Jim Boice and Roger Nicole, I kept my lips sealed. I did not want them to know how ignorant I was, so I just nodded like I understood what was going on.

Pastors have abandoned their high calling and substituted it with lesser functions. Their success, reputation, and sense of accomplishment is achieved by musical content, fashion, novelty, personality, and marketing savvy. Rarely do you find a pastor known as a theologian—as a biblical scholar. Rarely are there minds given to the mastery of Scripture and its doctrinal truth. Sadly, it is a difficult time for those who do understand their calling and who are experts in the interpretation, exposition, and doctrine of the Bible, because they are considered to be an anomaly. This has to change. Pastors must become theologians, biblical scholars, and guardians of sound doctrine.

In reality, de facto pastors are the theologians of the church, not the professors in institutions. The church understands theology from their pastor, and not from professional academics. Sinclair Ferguson said, "We have made little or no impression on the world for the very reason that gospel doctrine has made a correspondingly slight impression on us."[1] That is a tragic reality. Every significant pastor in church history, the names of whom you know, has been a heavyweight in theology. They all developed pastoral training institutions because the highest form of matured ecclesiology is the multiplication of pastor-theologians.

It was around 1650 that the Westminster Confession was developed. There were 121 scholars that spent years refining that great confession. They were the brightest minds, the theological heavyweights, and the biblical scholars of their day. Of the 121, all of them were pastors. We need to take theology back in the church. The academy has proven to be a very unsafe place for the Bible, and we need to take it back.

The academy started taking over after the Enlightenment took theology away from the church, and since the nineteenth century, pastors have been steadily forfeiting scholarly biblical theological influence. In our lifetime, the pastors who recognize the need to correct this travesty have all been working to salvage the Bible from academia.

Theology's Significance

How important is theology? The word itself means a divine propositional truth revealed in Scripture, which is the pastor's stock-in-trade. Doctrine is the foundation of absolutely everything. Doctrine is the structure of one's beliefs and convictions—the things that control our lives.

In 2 Corinthians 5, Paul made an interesting comment as he described what motivated him. We all understand how much the apostle endured for the sake of Christ, how much he suffered, and how challenging his ministry was. As he neared the end of his life, he wrote that even everyone in

Asia had forsaken him. The agonies that he went through are laid out in 2 Corinthians. We look at a man like that and ask, "What drove him? What moved him and kept him on course?" The answer is given in this statement: "The love of Christ controls us" (verse 14). It was the love of Christ that drove Paul.

If you were to ask most people about this today, they would say God loves everyone in the world equally and unconditionally. So what is Paul talking about? He explained, "Having concluded this, that one died for all, therefore all died; and He died for all, so that they who live might no longer live for themselves, but for Him who died and rose again on their behalf" (verses 14-15). Those two verses teach particular redemption—limited atonement. Jesus died for the all who died in Him. Paul was saying that his motivation was not that the death of Jesus Christ was some kind of potential expression of love, but that Christ died and rose for Paul personally. It was the apostle's understanding of particular redemption and a limited atonement that motivated him. He was Christ's!

Does theology matter? Does it change how you view life? Yes! But sadly, the church has doctrinal anemia, and that is why so many pastors who are considered to be successful have no interest in it.

Theological Revival from John 17

My concern is to help you to think about theology. To do that, let's look to John 17. Deep into the darkness of the Friday morning of Passion Week, Judas was already gathering the group that would come into the Garden of Gethsemane. Jesus had left the upper room, gone through Jerusalem to the east, and was heading toward the garden, where He would be arrested, and later that day, crucified. He had given promises and warnings to His disciples through chapters 13, 14, 15, and 16. Then, in their presence so they could hear, Jesus prayed the words of John 17. It is a breathtaking experience to read that prayer.

Back in Exodus 28, God had established the tabernacle, the priesthood, and even went so far as to define the clothing that the high priest was to wear. The priest was to put on a garment that represented the 12 tribes of Israel so that when he went in to the Holy of Holies to offer atonement on the Day of Atonement, and to offer incense as a symbol of prayers, he carried on his shoulders and over his heart the people of God, Israel.

That is exactly what happened in John 17. The great high priest, the Lord Jesus Christ, had gone into the heavenly holy of holies and was carrying His beloved people on His shoulders and on His heart. He did this in the presence of the Father. In the Old Testament, the high priest went into the Holy of Holies on the Day of Atonement and came out rapidly. But Christ went in, sat down, and He is still there. We are reminded in Hebrews 7 that He is ever living to make intercession for us—He is praying us into heaven. And John 17 depicts for us the present work of the Lord Jesus. Hebrews tells us that He is doing it; John 17 shows us His very words.

This high priestly prayer is the greatest ministry of the Lord Jesus Christ.

It is sad to me, given the incomparable uniqueness of this event, how it has been diminished in the church. I don't know that I've ever heard a sermon on John 17. We love to talk about the cross. We love to talk about the death of Christ and His resurrection—and we should. We love to talk about the cross and the resurrection as the fulfillment of prophecy, as actual history recorded in the Gospels, and as it is reflected on by the New Testament writers. I submit that both of those glorious events—the death and the resurrection of Christ—fall below the reality of John 17. This high priestly prayer is the greatest ministry of the Lord Jesus Christ. Does that surprise you? If you want to contemplate something that will contribute to your sanctification, you need to learn this work of Jesus.

"Much More Then"

Paul wrote in his letter to the Romans, "Therefore, having been justified by faith, we have peace with God through our Lord Jesus Christ, through whom also we have obtained our introduction by faith into this grace in which we stand; and we exult in hope of the glory of God" (Romans 5:1-2). The focus of this text is that we have been justified.

Paul went on to write, "For while we were still helpless, at the right time Christ died for the ungodly. For one will hardly die for a righteous man; though perhaps for the good man someone would dare even to die. But God demonstrates His own love toward us, in that while we were yet sinners, Christ died for us" (verses 6-8). We love that truth of the cross, and we must!

Now look at the first words of verse 9: "Much more then…" Much more than the cross? "Much more then, having now been justified by His blood, we shall be saved from the wrath of God through Him." Paul declared that having now been justified by Jesus' blood, "we shall [continue to] be saved from the wrath of God through Him." The apostle went on, "For if while we were enemies we were reconciled to God through the death of His Son, much more, having been reconciled, we shall be saved by His life" (verse 10).

Paul's comparison is that though the cross and resurrection of Jesus is an amazing truth, there is more to our salvation, which is the truth that we are being saved by His life. In verse 15, the apostle wrote, "The free gift is not like the transgression. For if by the transgression of the one the many died, much more did the grace of God and the gift by the grace of the one Man, Jesus Christ, abound to the many." Paul was comparing Adam to Christ, and he used the same exact words that we just read earlier in verse 9: "much more."

Verse 17 says, "If by the transgression of the one, death reigned through the one, much more those who receive the abundance of grace and of the gift of righteousness will reign in life through the One, Jesus Christ." Understand that the work of Christ is much more, comparatively speaking, than the work of Adam. We acknowledge how significant that "much more" is. And as the work of Christ is much more than what Adam did, so what Christ does for us alive is much more than His death.

Hebrews 9:12-14 reads,

> Not through the blood of goats and calves, but through His own blood, He entered the holy place once for all, having

obtained eternal redemption. For if the blood of goats and bulls and the ashes of a heifer sprinkling those who have been defiled sanctify for the cleansing of the flesh, how much more will the blood of Christ, who through the eternal Spirit offered Himself without blemish to God, cleanse your conscience from dead works to serve the living God?

Christ's sacrifice is much more than the animal sacrifices. Christ is much more than Adam, and so the work of Christ, who ever lives to bring us to glory, is much more than the work of the cross. He died in hours. He rose in days. He ever lives to make intercession!

Hebrews 7:23-25 should help solidify this truth: "The former priests, on the one hand, existed in greater numbers because they were prevented by death from continuing, but Jesus, on the other hand, because He continues forever, holds His priesthood permanently. Therefore He is able also to save forever those who draw near to God through Him, since He always lives to make intercession for them."

How does this escape us? And in light of this truth, all of a sudden John 17 becomes a precious treasure of incalculable value. This is Jesus' intermediary mediating ministry. In John 17 we meet the mediator, the Lord Jesus Christ Himself, and here He prays for His people.

Comfort in Theology

The entire prayer in John 17 is theology and doctrine. Apparently, if you do not have theology, not only can you not preach, you can't even pray. Here we find Jesus basing His entire ministry of intercession on sound doctrine; He pleads doctrine before His Father. This portion of Scripture is essentially a prayed systematic theological document on soteriology. And why would we expect anything less of Jesus, since He is the truth? Jesus prayed in the hearing of the 11 and all of us, for He wants all of us to understand this prayer.

We read in John 17:13, "Now I come to You; and these things I speak in the world so that they may have My joy made full in themselves." There is only one reason this prayer is here: for the Christian's joy. We know that the disciples that night needed a lot of joy. This is the Christ who comforts all of us with sound doctrine. He prays the theology of the Father back to the Father, knowing the Father will answer.

For whom does He pray this? Verse 9 says, "I ask on their behalf; I do not ask on behalf of the world, but of those whom You have given Me; for they are Yours." Jesus asked on behalf of the disciples and all those who believed. Also in verse 20: "I do not ask on behalf of these alone, but for those also who believe in Me through their word." Jesus prayed for all believers—those present at that time, and those who would follow through the rest of redemptive history. I am convinced that this is the most comforting chapter in the Bible because the security of the Christian's salvation is the most comforting truth we can know.

Into the Holy of Holies

Let us go into the holy of holies here and listen to the divine theologian praying us into heaven. This prayer is a preview of what Jesus would be doing after His ascension until the end of redemptive history. It reveals a transition from His earthly ministry to believers to His heavenly ministry for believers. The requests we find in John 17 have been offered constantly by Jesus for the last 2000 years, and He will continue to offer them until all of God's children are safely in heaven. This is the real Lord's Prayer, because only He could pray it. The prayer in Matthew 6 is not the Lord's Prayer, it is the Disciples' Prayer because the Lord could not pray it. He could not say, "Forgive us our transgressions," for He never sinned. John 17 is the Lord's Prayer, and the Lord prayed in the opening verses for the Father to bring Him to heaven—to bring Him safely through the dramatic events that were going to take place immediately after this time of prayer.

John 17:1-5 is a prayer for Jesus' own glory. He asked to be glorified so that He could be put in place to intercede for the redeemed. From verse 6 to the end of the chapter, He lifts an intercessory prayer for believers—for us. And this mediating ministry of Jesus Christ is going on even at this very moment. We see here the theology from the perfect theologian with absolutely perfect theology.

Salvation and the Trinity

Salvation begins with the doctrine of God, and Jesus teaches us about the Father in His prayer. We read in John 17:11, "Holy Father," and verse

25, "righteous Father." In verse 3 we learn that there is only one true God, the only eternal noncontingent being, and no one is like Him; everything else is contingent and dependent on Him for existence. However, to say that God is righteous, holy, and the only God does not inherently compel any act of kindness toward anyone. This is where there has been confusion recently regarding God and Allah. They are not the same. For Allah has been designed as a single solitary eternal being, not a trinity, who by virtue of his eternal singleness cannot love because there has never been anyone to love. Forever he has been one and only one. Allah possesses no relational attributes. How could he be loving when he is a single solitary person everlastingly? Allah is a form of the devil, and that is why there is no love, grace, mercy, and compassion in Islam.

In verses 23 and 24 of this chapter, Jesus made an amazing statement as He spoke to the Father: "I in them and You in Me, that they may be perfected in unity, so that the world may know that You sent Me, and loved them, even as You have loved Me. Father, I desire that they also, whom You have given Me, be with Me where I am, so that they may see My glory which You have given Me, for You loved Me before the foundation of the world." He continued in verse 26, "And I have made Your name known to them, and will make it known, so that the love with which You loved Me may be in them, and I in them." Jesus was saying that the definition of relationship in the Trinity is everlasting love. The true God is love because the true God has always loved.

There is more about the doctrine of God in verse 1: "Father, the hour has come; glorify Your Son, that the Son may glorify You." Here we meet the eternal Son. Again in verse 5: "Father, glorify Me together with Yourself, with the glory which I had with You before the world was." Now we know that the Father and the Son are defined by a loving relationship that has been from all eternity. The Father and the Son share an eternal nature, eternal love, and eternal glory.

That is why John began his Gospel account, "In the beginning was the Word, and the Word was with God, and the Word was God. He was in the beginning with God. All things came into being through Him, and apart from Him nothing came into being that has come into being" (John 1:1-3). In verse 14 of that same chapter he wrote, "And the Word became flesh, and dwelt among us, and we saw His glory, glory as of the only begotten from the Father, full of grace and truth." Then in verse 18 we read, "No one has seen God at any time; the only begotten God who is in the bosom of the Father, He has explained Him." The apostle Paul also understood this when he explained that in Christ "are hidden all the treasures of wisdom and knowledge" (Colossians 2:3); "in Him all the fullness of Deity dwells in bodily form" (2:9).

The foundation of salvation is a triune, holy, eternal, and loving God. A single god with no capacity to love has no interest in saving anyone. But the God of the Bible is defined by love. Jesus is pre-existent with God, co-existent with God, and self-existent with God.

In John 17, the Son was asking to be taken back to heaven and back to the eternal unity, love, and glory that He everlastingly had shared with the Father. It is as if Jesus was saying, "Father, take Me back because of who I am. You gave Me authority over all flesh; You have allowed Me to give eternal life. This is who I am. I am the eternal life because of what I've done. I've glorified You on the earth. I've accomplished the work You gave Me to do. Now take Me back." Here is the real personhood of the Trinity being demonstrated. Salvation exists because God is triune and God is love.

Another stunning statement about the nature of God is found in John 17:10: "All things that are Mine are Yours, and Yours are Mine." As mere mortals, we could join in the first part of this verse and say, "All things that are mine are Yours," but we could not say the second half: "All things that are Yours are mine." The only being who could make that statement is God.

The doctrines of salvation begin in the relationship of the Father and the Son in the Trinity. Paul wrote to Timothy about this God "who has saved us and called us with a holy calling, not according to our works, but according to His own purpose and grace which was granted us in Christ Jesus from all eternity" (2 Timothy 1:9). Redemptive history began as a plan within the Trinity, and because God is love, He desired to bring to Himself many more sons to love.

Salvation and Election

The second important doctrine within soteriology is the doctrine of election. The people to whom the eternal Son gives eternal life are clearly identified. Jesus said in John 17:2, "He may give eternal life." To whom does He give that eternal life? He gave us the answer in verse 9: "I do not ask on behalf of the world." Jesus was uniquely praying for all whom the Father had given to Him (John 17:2). Then in verse 11, Jesus used the same language: "Holy Father, keep them in Your name, the name which You have given Me." As clearly as the Father has given a name to the Son, He has given people to the Son.

This is not the first occurrence of this truth in John's Gospel. In John 6:37, Jesus said, "All that the Father gives Me will come to Me, and the one who comes to Me I will certainly not cast out." It is important to note that all the Father gives to Jesus will come to Him, and those who come to Him, He will not reject. This falls into the category of what theologians have called irresistible grace. Why? "For I have come down from heaven, not to do My own will, but the will of Him who sent Me. This is the will of Him who sent Me, that of all that He has given Me I lose nothing, but raise it up on the last day" (verses 38-39). Again He said in verse 44, "No one can come to Me unless the Father who sent Me draws him; and I will raise him up on the last day." Then again in verse 65: "For this reason I have said to you, that no one can come to Me unless it has been granted him from the Father." This is the doctrine of divine sovereign election.

How did God choose whom He would give to Jesus? The only answer to that is found in two places. First, John 17:6 says, "I have manifested Your name to the men whom You gave Me out of the world; they were Yours and You gave them to Me." Then in John 17:9 we read, "I ask on their behalf; I do not ask on behalf of the world, but of those whom You have given Me; for they are Yours." Believers belong to God based on His sovereign decree and uninfluenced choice. This is clearly what is meant when Scripture says, "He chose us in Him before the foundation of the world" (Ephesians 1:4).

The book of Revelation contains a reference about certain names written, from before the foundation of the world, in the Lamb's book of life. The Father draws them at the appropriate time in history and gives them as a love gift to the Son. The Son receives them, and then His responsibility is to make sure they get to glory, and that is why He incessantly prays us into heaven. For every purpose of God there is a means. The purpose of God is to bring us to glory, and the means is the intercession of Jesus Christ. Jesus said in John 17:9, "I ask on their behalf." Jesus prays for those who are the Father's by choice—He does not ask for the world. Then in verse 20 we read, "I do not ask on behalf of these alone, but for those also who believe in Me through their word." Jesus' prayer stretches through all of redemptive history.

Now, there are many people who say, "Christ died for the whole world." If Christ died for the entire world, then His will was at odds with the Father's. For the Father willed to save those whom He chose; therefore, Christ could not have died for the whole world or He would have been out of the will of the Father. It would be like saying the Father was a Calvinist and the Son was an Arminian, which is audacious, for there is only one will in the Trinity. Jesus does not pray for those who are not the Father's, nor did He die for those who are not the Father's.

What about Judas? John 17:12 explains, "While I was with them, I was keeping them in Your name which You have given Me; and I guarded them and not one of them perished but the son of perdition, so that the Scripture would be fulfilled." Judas was not an exception, for he did exactly what Scripture said he would do. He never was a son of God; he was always a son of destruction and damnation.

God is defined as love, and His love is so vast that it stretches beyond even the fulfillment of loving the Son and the Spirit. He wants many sons to love, and so He chooses them, gives them to the Son, and the Son grants them eternal life and intercedes for them.

Salvation and the Incarnation

For all of this to have taken place, sinners needed a Savior, for the Father could not bring unrighteous people to heaven. That leads to the third doctrine—the doctrine of the incarnation. We have already seen the deity of Christ indicated as we looked at the Trinity, but we also see His humanity in John 17. In verse 8 Jesus said, "I came forth from You." That is the incarnation, the virgin birth. Similarly, in verse 3 we read, "Jesus Christ whom You have sent." Then again in verse 18, "As You sent Me into the world"; verse 21, "You sent Me"; verse 23, "You sent Me," and verse 25, "You sent Me."

Nearly 30 times in the Gospel of John, Jesus said He was sent by the Father. He indicated His humanity again in John 17:4: "I glorified You on the earth, having accomplished the work which You have given Me to do." And in verse 13, He anticipated returning back through the ascension. There are indications all through this chapter of Jesus' deity and humanity.

More importantly, consider also His work. In verse 4 Jesus prayed, "I glorified You on the earth, having accomplished the work which You have given Me to do." Understanding the incarnation entails you to understand not only the nature of Christ, but also the work of Christ. He was given the task of providing eternal life to the chosen, and by what work would He do that? There were two necessary realities.

Atonement

First, Jesus had to make atonement for sins. Theologians call this passive righteousness. He came to give His life a ransom for many. He bore in His own body our sins: "He was pierced through for our transgressions, He was crushed for our iniquities" (Isaiah 53:5). He had to die as a substitutionary sacrifice for His bride. He had to pay the price of death in order to satisfy the Father's justice, propitiating the Father. And then He was raised from the dead as the Father validated His sacrifice. He had to die, but He also had to live.

Righteousness

Second, notice Jesus said in John 17:4, "I glorified You on the earth." The Father affirmed that the Son had done just that when He spoke, "This is My beloved Son, in whom I am well-pleased" (Matthew 3:17). Jesus did nothing but glorify God on earth; He was holy, harmless, and undefiled. In John 17:19 we read, "For their sakes I sanctify Myself." That is a powerful statement regarding active righteousness. Jesus lived a perfect life in order for that full life to be credited to our account. He died a substitutionary death so that death could be credited to our account. This is the substitutionary work of Jesus Christ passively and actively.

Then in verse 12 He added, "While I was with them, I was keeping them in Your name which You have given Me; and I guarded them and not one of them perished." While Jesus was on earth, He was living a perfectly righteous life that would be credited to His followers. He was going to die a substitutionary death for sinners. And throughout that entire process, He was also protecting and securing His own.

Often we get the idea that because the Lord says we are secure and our salvation is forever, it just automatically happens. Yet there are divine means the Lord had for guarding His own while He was on earth. Because He sanctified Himself and lived a righteous life to be credited to the people whom God had chosen, because He died a substitutionary death and satisfied the justice of God in the place of sinners, He was given authority over all flesh to give eternal life. As Jesus said to the Father in John 17:3, "This is eternal life, that they may know You, the only true God, and Jesus Christ whom You have sent."

In summary, salvation is to know God, to know Christ. This knowledge comes from the theology revealed to us in His Word. May we once again be reminded that theology is not merely optional.

PRAYER

Lord, we are so blessed to have been able to reach down into this incredible portion of Scripture and pull up some of the richness in it. To look back at the cross and what Christ did and to contemplate the resurrection is a wonderful thing, but how much more exhilarating and comforting is it to know that this very moment He is alive at Your right hand, Father, praying us into heaven. What a sanctifying realization! Accomplish Your perfect purpose in every life, we pray, for the sake of our Savior. Amen.

THE LORD'S GREATEST PRAYER, PART 2

"Sanctify them in the truth; Your word is truth."

JOHN 17:17

2

THE LORD'S GREATEST PRAYER, PART 2

John MacArthur

Shepherds' Conference 2016

John 17

As pastors, we need to take up the duty of being biblical scholars and theologians. By that I mean we are to know the Word of God well enough so that we can communicate it effectively to God's people. The example of a theological mind, of course, is our own Lord Jesus Christ. In John 17 we see how theology essentially governed everything that He said, not only in His preaching, but also in His praying. The book of Hebrews has much to say about the Lord Jesus Christ as our great high priest, but only in John 17 do we have a sample of that mediating intercessory ministry. This is the only example in Scripture of what He has been doing in heaven incessantly since His ascension.

This intercessory work is of utmost importance—not to say that we diminish in any way the significance of the cross or the resurrection. However, the cross was accomplished in hours, the resurrection in days, but several thousand years have already passed in the course of His intercessory work. We read in Hebrews 7:25, "He always lives to make intercession for them." For 2000 years, Jesus has been praying us into heaven against the force of sin that assails us. We get a sample of this in the darkness of the Friday morning of Passion Week as Jesus was about to enter the Garden of Gethsemane to be arrested and then crucified. He prayed this prayer in the hearing of the 11, and on behalf of them. But according to John 17:20, He was praying not only for them, "but for those also who believe in Me through their word." He was praying for believers in all the rest of redemptive history, and His prayer is soteriological doctrine.

As we have already seen, the gospel begins with God, and our Lord's prayer started with God; He spoke to the holy and righteous Father. We observed in the prayer that God is triune. Therefore, God is love, because eternally there has been relationship between the Father, Son, and Spirit, and that relationship is defined by an incomprehensible, infinite, and intimate love. Second, we noticed that embedded in this prayer are multiple statements about the doctrine of election. And third, we witnessed in this prayer the doctrine of the incarnation—the Father had sent Jesus into the world. Jesus said in verse 4, "I glorified You on the earth, having accomplished the work which You have given Me to do."

Divine Revelation

There is yet another doctrine that this prayer teaches us—the doctrine of revelation. The elect for whom Christ died and lived have to believe the gospel to be saved. If there is no gospel, there is no salvation. And that gospel must be presented in an unalterable and fixed way. Truth has to be delivered to the world so that it can be preached throughout the rest of redemptive history. We see in Jesus' high priestly prayer that the Son has delivered this truth. Read verse 6: "I have manifested Your name to the men whom You gave Me." Jesus revealed God to the disciples. He revealed God's will to them, for He did only what His Father told Him to do. The Son's food was to do the will of Him who sent Him (John 4:34). And He manifested the fullness of who the Father is.

In John 17:26, right at the very end of the chapter, Jesus said essentially the same thing: "I have made Your name known to them, and will make it known." He will keep on revealing God through all of redemptive history. How did He—and how does He continue to—reveal God and make His name known?

First, Jesus revealed God in His person. In John 1:14 we read, "The Word became flesh, and dwelt among us, and we saw His glory, glory as of the only begotten from the Father, full of grace and truth." In verse 18 we are told, "No one has seen God at any time; the only begotten God who is in the bosom of the Father, He has explained Him." A synonym for "explained" is *exegete*. Jesus has exegeted the Father. Jesus went so far as to say, in John 12:45, "He who sees Me sees the One who sent Me." Again in John 14:9, "He who has seen Me has seen the Father."

We read in Colossians, "In Him all the fullness of Deity dwells in bodily form" (2:9). In Hebrews 1:3 we read, "He is the radiance of His glory and the exact representation of His nature."

Jesus revealed God in His person, and He also revealed God in His words. For example, in John 12:44-50 we read,

> Jesus cried out and said, "He who believes in Me, does not believe in Me but in Him who sent Me. He who sees Me sees the One who sent Me. I have come as Light into the world, so that everyone who believes in Me will not remain in darkness. If anyone hears My sayings and does not keep them, I do not judge him; for I did not come to judge the world, but to save the world. He who rejects Me and does not receive My sayings, has one who judges him; the word I spoke is what will judge him at the last day. For I did not speak on My own initiative, but the Father Himself who sent Me has given Me a commandment as to what to say and what to speak. I know that His commandment is eternal life; therefore the things I speak, I speak just as the Father has told Me."

Jesus is the inherent, infallible, and divine revelation of God. In John 17:8, He said, "The words which You gave Me I have given to them; and they received them and truly understood that I came forth from You, and they believed that You sent Me." In verse 14 He said, "I have given them Your word."

Though Jesus clearly had a commitment to the Old Testament—in the Gospels, there are about 80 instances in which He made reference to different Old Testament books…27 of them—He also knew that what He was saying was new revelation. Jesus knew the power of the New Testament when He said in John 17:17, "Sanctify them in the truth; Your word is truth." He was not only reaching back to the Scriptures that had already been written, but He was looking forward to what would be written—that which would be absolutely essential for the sanctification of His people—so that they may be, as verse 19 states, "sanctified in truth."

Our Lord had already, on that very night, acknowledged the role of the Holy Spirit in the coming days. He said in John 14:16-17, "I will ask the Father, and He will give you another Helper, that He may be with you forever; that is the Spirit of truth, whom the world cannot receive, because it does not see Him or know Him, but you know Him because He abides with you and will be in you." We learn more from verse 26: "The Helper, the Holy Spirit, whom the Father will send in My name, He will teach you all things, and bring to your remembrance all that I said to you." That is why the apostles and their associates were able to record their Gospel accounts and be absolutely inerrant and accurate.

John 15:26-27 reads, "When the Helper comes, whom I will send to you from the Father, that is the Spirit of truth who proceeds from the Father, He will testify about Me." In 16:12-13 we see, "I have many more things to say to you, but you cannot bear them now. But when He, the Spirit of truth, comes, He will guide you into all the truth; for He will not speak on His own initiative, but whatever He hears, He will speak; and He will disclose to you what is to come." Again, in verse 15, "All things that the Father has are Mine; therefore I said that He takes of Mine and will disclose it to you."

The truth was passed down from the Father, to the Son, to the Spirit, to the apostles. The Father, the Son, and the Spirit are truth. Our Lord had a clear view of revelation and the integrity of Scripture. This revelation is directly associated with salvation, because our transformation depends on what is completely external to all of us: The incarnate Son declared His gospel.

In Romans 10:13-15 we have the familiar necessity of preaching articulated perhaps more clearly than anywhere else: "'Whoever will call on the name of the Lord will be saved.' How then will they call on Him in whom they have not believed? How will they believe in Him whom they have not heard? And how will they hear without a preacher? How will they preach unless they are sent? Just as it is written, 'How beautiful are the feet of those who bring good news of good things!'" We continue in verse 17, "Faith comes from hearing, and hearing by the word of Christ." That is why Peter wrote in 1 Peter 1:23, "You have been born again not of seed which is perishable but imperishable, that is, through the living and enduring word of God."

In John 17:8 Jesus explained that the disciples had received the Word, understood the Word, and believed the Word. Consequently, that is what marks the faith that saves. This revelation from God not only has the power for salvation, but also for sanctification. "Sanctify them in the truth; Your word is truth" (verse 17). The Spirit of Christ has inspired the Scripture, and the Scripture stands forever. When a person receives, understands, and believes, that person receives eternal life from the Son.

Regeneration

That leads to the next doctrine in this string of pearls: the doctrine of regeneration, or the work of God that makes repentance and belief possible. We were born in darkness, blindness, ignorance, and inescapable sin. Thus, we have to be made spiritually alive.

John 3 records an interesting conversation Jesus had with Nicodemus. The religious leader came to the Lord because he had a question on his heart different from the one on his lips. Nicodemus wanted to know how to be born again, how to enter the kingdom of God. Jesus responded in verse 3, "Truly, truly, I say to you, unless one is born again he cannot see the kingdom of God."

Nicodemus's reply is found in verse 4: "How can a man be born when he is old?"

Jesus' answer is amazing: "Truly, truly, I say to you, unless one is born of water and the Spirit he cannot enter into the kingdom of God. That which is born of the flesh is flesh, and that which is born of the Spirit is spirit. Do not be amazed that I said to you, 'You must be born again'" (verses 5-7).

Notice we still haven't seen an answer to the question "How?" In verse 8, Jesus said, "The wind blows where it wishes and you hear the sound of it, but do not know where it comes from and where it is going; so is everyone who is born of the Spirit." What a strange answer. Jesus explained to Nicodemus that salvation is the Spirit's work—and He does it to whom He wills, when He wills.

In John 17:2-3 we read, "He may give eternal life. This is eternal life, that they may know You, the only true God, and Jesus Christ whom You have sent." Eternal life is a present reality, and to have it is to know God, know Christ, and to come out of death, darkness, ignorance, alienation, and blindness into life and light. It is to move, as Paul would put it, from being a natural man who understands not the things of God to someone who has the mind of Christ.

In John 10:27, Jesus stated, "My sheep hear My voice, and I know them, and they follow Me." And we find out something else in John 8:19: "So they were saying to Him, 'Where is Your Father?' Jesus answered, 'You know neither Me nor My Father; if you knew Me, you would know My Father also.'" It is a package deal. If you do not know both the Father and the Son, you do not know either.

What is eternal life? It is the true transforming knowledge of God. First John 5:20 reads, "We know that the Son of God has come, and has given us understanding so that we may know Him who is true; and we are in Him who is true, in His Son Jesus Christ. This is the true God and eternal life." Eternal life is not something God gives you; it is you being in God, and God being in you. In being regenerate, you have been drawn up into the realm in which Christ exists. You have been removed from the world. That is why Jesus said,

> If you were of the world, the world would love its own; but because you are not of the world, but I chose you out of the world, because of this the world hates you. Remember the word that I said to you, "A slave is not greater than his master." If they persecuted Me, they will also persecute you; if they kept My word, they will keep yours also. But all these things they will do to you for My name's sake, because they do not know the One who sent Me (John 15:19-21).

The world and the kingdom of Christ are two colliding kingdoms. And when you have been regenerated, you have been drawn up and out of the world. That is why verses 24-25 read, "If I had not done among them the works which no one else did, they would not have sin; but now they have both seen and hated Me and My Father as well. But they have done this to fulfill the word that is written in their Law, 'They hated Me without a cause.'"

But as regenerated children who are no longer a part of the world, we still have a job in the world:

> I tell you the truth, it is to your advantage that I go away; for if I do not go away, the Helper will not come to you; but if I go, I will send Him to you. And He, when He comes, will convict the world concerning sin and righteousness and judgment; concerning sin, because they do not believe in Me; and concerning righteousness, because I go to the Father and you no longer see Me; and concerning judgment, because the ruler of this world has been judged (John 16:7-11).

You may be thinking, *How does that have any relationship to me at all?* John 17:18 gives us the answer: "As you sent Me into the world, I also have sent them into the world." Christ came to save sinners, not the righteous. He came to preach the gospel, and then gave us the task to keep preaching the gospel to this world. The Holy Spirit's internal work of conviction that sends sinners fleeing to the Savior is a mandate for the character of our evangelism. We are God's prosecutors. As a Christian, you indict sinners. Ephesians 5:11 explains how this takes place: "Do not participate in the unfruitful deeds of darkness, but instead even expose them." We expose and indict sinners. First Corinthians 14:24 affirms this: "If all prophesy, and an unbeliever or an ungifted man enters, he is convicted by all, he is called to account by all." If you are not prosecuting sinners, you are not doing your job.

In the Old Testament, indictment, conviction, and prosecution were the dominant features of the forensic ministry of the prophets. Jude 14-15 affirms this: "It was also about these men that Enoch, in the seventh generation from Adam, prophesied, saying, 'Behold, the Lord came with many thousands of His holy ones, to execute judgment upon all, and to convict all the ungodly of all their ungodly deeds which they have done in an ungodly way, and of all the harsh things which ungodly sinners have spoken against Him.'"

That is not how people preach today. Old Testament prophets were

God's prosecutors. John the Baptist was God's last Old Testament prose-cutor, and it cost him his head. Jesus indicted Israel by telling them a par-able about a man who kept killing the messengers who came back to his vineyard, and finally the man sent his son, and they killed him. The Jew-ish leaders killed Jesus because He stressed their unrighteous state. After we experience regeneration, we instantaneously become the prosecutors of the world. This has to be a vital part of our ministry, for the gospel must be seen as a rescue from damnation.

There is, of course, a positive side to regeneration. In John 17:10, Jesus said, "I have been glorified in them." Before we were regenerated, we fell short of God's glory. Now that we have been regenerated, He is glorified in us. The glory of God shining in the face of Jesus Christ becomes embod-ied in us, and we become the temple of the Lord Himself. At the same time, we are ripped out of the world, and we are so alien to it that it is vio-lently hostile toward us.

Union with Christ

That leads us to a sixth doctrine in Jesus' high priestly prayer, and that is the doctrine of union with Christ. The reality of eternal life involves a real union with the Trinity. In John 17:11, Jesus asked the Father "that they may be one." This is not some kind of superficial unity, for Jesus specified that His followers be one "even as We are." The Trinity does not have trou-ble getting along. The verse is not trying to communicate to us that if we work hard enough, we can kind of get along with each other. What Jesus is talking about here is ontological, not experiential. He is talking about being one in the common life of God.

In verse 21 Jesus prays "that they may all be one; even as You, Father, are in Me and I in You, that they also may be in Us." He prays further about this unity in verse 23: "I in them and You in Me, that they may be perfected in unity." It feels as though we are getting lost in the Trinity. It is the Father and the Son, and the Son and the Father, and the Spirit in both, the Spirit in us, and us in the Spirit. This union is so powerful that the result is this: "that the world may know that You sent Me" (verse 23).

> **Being one with God is infinitely more joyous,
> infinitely more blessed than all the riches
> and comforts of this world.**

This is such a staggering concept to understand, the profound reality of what salvation brings. In John 14:16-20, Jesus said,

> I will ask the Father, and He will give you another Helper, that He may be with you forever; that is the Spirit of truth, whom the world cannot receive, because it does not see Him or know Him, but you know Him because He abides with you and will be in you. I will not leave you as orphans; I will come to you. After a little while the world will no longer see Me, but you will see Me; because I live, you will live also. In that day you will know that I am in My Father, and you in Me, and I in you.

This is absolutely overwhelming. We have the privilege of being wrapped up in the Trinity. We share the same life. "Jesus answered and said to him, 'If anyone loves Me, he will keep My word; and My Father will love him, and We will come to him and make Our abode with him'" (verse 23). Salvation is not just a ticket to heaven, not just the forgiveness of sins, and not just escape from judgment; salvation is being caught up in the eternal life of the Trinity. We know God, Christ, and the Holy Spirit not as distant or secondhand, but near and firsthand. We know the triune God not vaguely, as if unclear, but distinctly and without confusion. We know God not doubtfully as if insecure, but confidently and boldly.

Because of this oneness with God, sin must appear to us to be far more alien than we ever imagined. Maybe that will help you understand Paul's exhortation in 1 Corinthians 6:19: "Do you not know that your body is a temple of the Holy Spirit who is in you, whom you have from God, and that you are not your own?" You are inseparable from the triune God. Being one with God is infinitely more joyous, infinitely more blessed than all the riches and comforts of this world. If it is not, then heaven will be less for you. If God is not all your joy here, then heaven will be less for you.

Sanctification

Union with the triune God must impact our lives. Though we are perfect in Christ positionally, Jesus still taught about the importance of sanctification. John 17:15 reads, "I do not ask You to take them out of the world." We are left on this earth, but Jesus is praying that the Father would "keep them from the evil one" (verse 15). We are safe in the eternal sense, but unsafe in the temporal sense, for we live in imminent danger. One of the most amazing statements in this entire chapter is in verse 16: "They are not of the world, even as I am not of the world." Jesus was saying that His disciples were as He was with reference to the world, but they had to stay on earth, for He was going to the Father and they were not. It is as if Jesus declared, "My work is done, but theirs is beginning."

For us believers who are left in the world, there are imminent dangers. First John 5:19 reads, "The whole world lies in the power of the evil one." The evil one, Satan, seeks to devour, deceive, and destroy. We are to resist him so that he flees. We are to arm ourselves so that we are not vulnerable. We are to be knowledgeable of his devices. This is summed up in John 17:17: "Sanctify them in the truth; Your word is truth." That can only happen through the Word, in the power of the Spirit. We have an example from Christ, in verse 19: "For their sakes I sanctify Myself, that they themselves also may be sanctified in truth." When Jesus stated that He had been sanctified in truth, He was saying He had been set apart from sin perfectly.

What does being set apart look like? Jesus said in John 4:34, "My food is to do the will of Him who sent Me and to accomplish His work." In John 5:19, He said, "Truly, truly, I say to you, the Son can do nothing of Himself, unless it is something He sees the Father doing; for whatever the Father does, these things the Son also does in like manner." And in John 5:30 He said, "I can do nothing on My own initiative."

We also read in John 6:38, "I have come down from heaven, not to do My own will, but the will of Him who sent Me." Again, in 7:18: "He who speaks from himself seeks his own glory; but He who is seeking the glory of the One who sent Him, He is true, and there is no unrighteousness in Him." Jesus sought God's glory and will while on earth.

Sanctification comes through obedience, and perfect obedience is perfect sanctification. Jesus sanctified Himself demonstrably—manifestly—by His perfect obedience. Sanctification is perfect obedience to the Word and will of God. By what power did He do this? Of course He was God, but everything He did in His incarnation was by the power of the Holy Spirit working through Him. What a perfect model for us—Jesus walked in the Spirit, and that is why His life was characterized by love, joy, peace, gentleness, goodness, faith, meekness, self-control, and never anything else.

Glorification

The final doctrine we find in Jesus' prayer is the doctrine of glorification. We see this truth multiple times in this one chapter. John 17:1 says, "Jesus spoke these things; and lifting up His eyes to heaven, He said, 'Father, the hour has come; glorify Your Son, that the Son may glorify You.'" Again in verse 5: "Now, Father, glorify Me together with Yourself, with the glory which I had with You before the world was." And in verse 24: "Father, I desire that they also, whom You have given Me, be with Me where I am, so that they may see My glory which You have given Me, for You loved Me before the foundation of the world."

Jesus wanted His followers to see what it looks like to be loved by the Father forever from before the foundation of the world. The whole intent of the redemptive work of Christ, and the intercession of the eternal Son, is to bring all those who were chosen by God's sovereign election, and were given to the Son as His bride, and have been used to preach and write and proclaim the Word of God, and who have believed the Word of God, and have been sanctified by the Word of God—to take all of these people who possess eternal life, whose sins have all been paid for by the Son's death, and whose lives are covered by His perfect righteousness—and bring them all to heaven.

Jesus said in verse 12, "While I was with them, I was keeping them in Your name which You have given Me; and I guarded them and not one of them perished." Back in verse 11 He said, "I am no longer in the world;

and yet they themselves are in the world, and I come to You. Holy Father, keep them in Your name." He will keep us till the end, and that wonderful truth is reaffirmed in Jude verse 24: "Now to Him who is able to keep you from stumbling, and to make you stand in the presence of His glory blameless with great joy." Guess what? We are all going to make it! We have an eternal salvation from the almighty God.

Why does God do all of this? Why save us, keep us, protect us, and bring us to eternal glory? Hours away from the cross, Jesus revealed His motivation for the suffering that stood in His path. In John 13:1 we find some of the most beautiful words you will ever hear: "Before the Feast of the Passover, Jesus knowing that His hour had come that He would depart out of this world to the Father, having loved His own who were in the world, He loved them to the end." He loved us to the end!

We have to admit that, as unredeemed sinners, we were not the most lovable people. But when God loves His own, He has only one way to love them, and that is infinitely. That infinite love was stated at the end of Jesus' prayer:

> I in them and You in Me, that they may be perfected in unity, so that the world may know that You sent Me, and loved them, even as You have loved Me. Father, I desire that they also, whom You have given Me, be with Me where I am, so that they may see My glory which You have given Me, for You loved Me before the foundation of the world (17:23-24).

I don't even know what to do with that amazing truth. Jesus wants to take us to glory so that we can see and know what it is to be eternally, intimately, and infinitely loved by the Father. How can the Father love us as He loved the Son? Because we are in His beloved Son. When the Bible says that God loves us, it is not speaking of a superficial love. The eternal and infinite God loves us intimately.

The Son prayed and continues to pray for us based on all these incomparably glorious doctrines in order to bring us into heaven—so that we will be loved forever in the same way the Father loves the eternal Son. In our role we must be like Christ and not only know and teach theology, but have it permeate us so thoroughly that we pray it as well.

PRAYER

Father, we thank You for these truths in Scripture that are beyond comprehension. We smile as our souls are just swept away. To be loved as Christ is loved? To be taken to glory so that we can be loved as He has always been loved? What a great plan, what a great salvation, what a great Savior!

Lord Jesus, even now, as You are interceding for us, we praise Your name. We thank You for Your unceasing vigilance to keep us from stumbling. You bring all of the Father's sons into the fullness of His eternal love. We are utterly unworthy of this, but Lord, may it speak to our hearts in such a way that not only does it bring joy and comfort, but it reminds us how alien sin is to those who live in the Triune God, and in whom the triune God lives. Use us to proclaim the glories of the gospel. We pray in our Savior's name. Amen.

ADAM, WHERE ART THOU?

"The LORD God planted a garden toward the east, in Eden;
and there He placed the man whom He had formed."

GENESIS 2:8

3

ADAM, WHERE ART THOU? REDISCOVERING THE HISTORICAL ADAM IN THE PAGES OF SCRIPTURE

William Barrick

Shepherds' Conference 2013

Selected Scriptures

The historicity of Adam is a debated topic as of late. Just within the last several months, there have been multiple articles and books published on the subject. Indeed, as I write, I am preparing to speak at a symposium on the issue. In fact, it seems that everywhere I go I find that people are interested in what has been labeled "Rediscovering the Historical Adam." It is confounding that this is the chosen title, because Adam has been there all along.

Back in the day when vehicles had bench seats, my wife used to sit next to me. As car design and safety regulations developed, the car manufacturers switched to bucket seats and seat belts. Now my wife sits on what feels like the other side of the car, and she'll occasionally mention that she misses sitting together. I say to her, "Well, I haven't moved." That is the way it is with the historical Adam. He has been there in the text all along, and it is something of a misnomer to suggest that we are "rediscovering him." If God is allowing Adam to see, from heaven, the discussion that's taking place now, he is probably wondering what is going on.

However, this discussion is necessary because some key questions have arisen: Was Adam the first of the human race? Or was he just the head of a clan, a tribe, or a nation? Maybe he was merely symbolic and not a real individual? Is he a product of evolution? If he is a product of evolution, what does that look like, and what are the implications for Eve? She has the same DNA as Adam, which makes sense if you take a part out of his side and use it to make a woman. But how does that work with evolution? I want to take some time and provide a biblical analysis of the historicity of Adam.

How Important Is Adam?

Duane Gish, a leader in the creationist movement, recently went home to be with his Lord and Savior at the age of 93. Years ago, he was speaking at a conference and said, "God and Adam were talking in the Garden of Eden. Adam said, 'Lord, I want a woman. She must be beautiful, charming, a good cook, a housekeeper, and willing to wait on me hand and foot.' God said, 'I can make you a woman like that, but it will cost an arm and leg.' Adam's response, 'What can I get for a rib?'"

Many of those who remember Duane Gish recall him telling that joke far better than I can. It relates to the crux of the problem: Namely, did Adam really exist? Many today suggest that the story of Adam is merely myth, legend, or allegory—spiritualized truth. People seem to be willing to accept miracles in the New Testament, as if God could do something special there through Jesus, but not so in the Old Testament. People do not struggle to accept the virgin birth as much as they do God creating the heavens, the earth, and a man.

Here at The Master's Seminary and Grace Community Church, we affirm that Adam was a historical person and the originating head of the entire human race. There was no man before him; there is no such thing as a pre-Adamite race. Indeed, when we look at the historical Adam, we see that his existence is essential to many areas of biblical understanding. The historical Adam is foundational to all creative activity, for if we cannot believe that God created Adam out of the dust of the ground and breathed into his nostrils the breath of life, then how can we believe that God created the universe?

The historical Adam is foundational to the history and nature of the human race. His existence determines our understanding of mankind—whether or not man is made in the image of God as a special creation, with a specific design distinct from all other parts of creation. The historical Adam is also directly connected to the origin and nature of sin. How is sin conceived in the human race if Adam is not its original head? If he is one of a thousand others—and there are supposedly fossil humanoids in the rocks dating prior to Adam—then how does his sin get attributed to those who lived before him?

The historical Adam is foundational to the existence and nature of human death. Paul said in Romans 5:12 that "through one man sin entered into the world, and death through sin." Therefore, the historical Adam is also foundational to the reality of salvation from sin. If the first Adam is merely allegorical, then what about the second Adam, Jesus Christ? If the second Adam is allegorical, then how is He capable of producing a literal sacrifice acceptable to God for the sins of mankind?

The historical Adam is foundational to the account of historical events in the book of Genesis. As Dr. MacArthur often says, if you don't accept the literal nature of the first chapters of Genesis, when do you start accepting the literal record of the Word of God? Thus the historical Adam is fundamental to the authority, inspiration, and inerrancy of the Bible.

Evaluating Presuppositions

There are certain presuppositions that we need to reject and others that we need to affirm when approaching this topic. First, we reject the concept of an old earth. The earth may be many thousands of years old, but it is not millions of years old.

Second, we also reject the documentary hypothesis—that the Torah can be divided up into various source documents like the JEDP (Jahwist, Elohist, Deuteronomist, Priestly) documents—and that it was composed and compiled over many centuries.

Third, we affirm that the author of Genesis is God Himself. This is evident from the creation account because there was no one else present other than God. We read that God said to Job, "Where were you when I laid the foundation of the earth?" (Job 38:4). His point was that if Job was there, then he would be God. If Job was God, then he would be able to create, to call the stars by name, to set the course of celestial bodies. Job was not able to do these things, nor was he able to see into the hearts of men, or judge mankind—he was not omniscient, omnipotent, or omnipresent. He was not God.

For that reason, Job was not able to deliver himself from his difficult circumstances or from the power, presence, and penalty of sin. Job had to put his hand over his mouth because he had been so busy trying to protect his own integrity that he was willing to impugn the integrity of God. God corrected Job's thinking—He is the ultimate author of the Scriptures, He was the eyewitness of creation, and it's His account that we have in Genesis 1.

Fourth, we affirm and uphold the independent historical accuracy of the Scriptures, from Genesis chapter 1 through Revelation chapter 22.

Fifth, we employ one consistent hermeneutic for interpreting all of Scripture. We don't change hermeneutics after Genesis 11. Instead, we use the same means of interpretation throughout.

Finally, we affirm the universal scope of Genesis 1 through 11—that is to say, it is pre-Israelite. Genesis 1 to 11 is not an exclusively Israelite book written for that nation alone. Moses penned it, but the record of the history of those chapters precedes Moses; it pertains to the time of the patriarchs. From where did Moses get the information? He may have had documents that were preserved that he could utilize (much like Luke used documents to write his Gospel), or God the Holy Spirit could have given Moses divine revelation, directly telling him what had occurred.

Regardless of how Moses obtained the information, the first 11 chapters of Genesis are not about Israel. This is where Old Testament scholar Peter Enns makes his mistake. He says that Adam is an Israelite, and that his story is about Israel, and it is for Israel.[1] This is not the case. Rather, Genesis 1–11 provides the foundation of the worldwide scope of salvation, redemption, and kingdom that God establishes and plans in His program. These chapters lay out God's design and purpose for all of mankind. They are universal in scope, for all people begin here, and all people are addressed here. In support of this, we observe that both the Old and the

New Testaments assume a common human origin in Adam. Considering first the Hebrew Scriptures, Malachi 2:10 says, "Do we not all have one father?" I believe the translators of the New American Standard update have rightly left father uncapitalized, for the prophet is not talking about God, but man. Mankind has one father—namely, Adam.

The New Testament teaches the same truth. In Acts 17:26, the apostle Paul said, "He made from one *man* every nation of mankind." The New American Standard update adds the word "man" in italics to indicate the referent. It becomes clear from the preceding verse what Paul is talking about: He explains that all mankind owes its existence to a God who created them and breathed the breath of life into them—into that one man. The context makes it very clear that the apostle is referring to the original man, Adam, and explaining that all of mankind is made from him.

Adam and Evolution

Oftentimes those who reject the historical Adam do so on the basis of evolutionary science. They affirm biological evolution such that they must jump through hoops to interpret the Scriptures differently from what the Scriptures appear to say. Evolution factors into many people's presuppositions when they approach the historicity of Adam—they begin with evolutionary science and the concept of an old earth, accepting the dictates of modern science. But just as with reading and interpreting Scripture, we must examine the evidence for scientific assertions and interpret them. We must not take the opinions of scientists as evidence itself. Rather, we must realize that they are presenting their interpretation of the evidence.

Was Israel a Prescientific Culture?

There are some who accuse Christians of ignoring the fact that Israel was a prescientific culture. They believe that the biblical writers had a rudimentary worldview; specifically, that the Israelites believed in a flat earth—a disk on top of the sea with a solid dome for the sky—a three-storied earth, as it were. They suggest that the sky was viewed as a vault resting on foundations, perhaps mountains, with doors and windows that let in the rain, and that God dwelt above the sky hidden in the clouds, and the world was secured or moored on the water by pillars. The earth was the only known domain; the realm beyond was considered unknowable. If the biblical writers had such a prescientific worldview, then the question is asked: How can we accept Scripture's account to be accurate when it has nothing to do with science or history?

By way of a response, we must question the presupposition. Is this an accurate portrayal of how the pre-Flood patriarchs viewed the world? Genesis 4 talks of metallurgy, of working with iron and of making musical instruments. That implies an ability to make music, the composition of which is sophisticated. The people referred to in Genesis 4 lived many hundreds of years before Israel came on the scene, but they were certainly not prescientific.

Literary Devices in the Ancient World

Also, critics say we must assume that the ancient Israelites had no understanding of literary devices—that they could not use similes, metaphors, and figures of speech. But in Job 9:6, Job speaks about God in this way: "Who shakes the earth out of its place, and its pillars tremble." Does Job refer to pillars literally or figuratively here? Later, in Job 26:7, Job said this of God: "He stretches out the north over empty space and hangs the earth on nothing." Either Job is contradicting himself—the earth hanging on nothing and yet on pillars—or he is employing a metaphor. Similarly, Job said, "My days are swifter than a weaver's shuttle, and come to an end without hope" (Job 7:6). Rather than take this as a literal statement, we should understand that Job was intelligent enough to use figures of speech.

If a man living contemporary or prior to the time of Abraham, before 2000 BC, had that capability, then why not the Israelites? Why could they not understand the use of metaphors? Indeed, it is somewhat anti-Semitic to suggest that the worldview of the Israelites must be interpreted apart from the use of metaphors, because we allow for such things in symbols written by the ancient Chinese, the ancient Sumerians, and the ancient Egyptians. We acknowledge such forms of communication with other cultures, but with respect to Israel 2000 years later, there seems to be a rejection of it.

Consider the fact that written language dating back to 1600 BC has been found on the walls of Egyptian mines from Serabit el-Khadim down in the Sinai Peninsula. That means the people were not only able to write, but to read and understand. Those inscriptions date to 200 years before Moses wrote the Pentateuch. Even the slaves were literate, and on those walls we find written the same name used for God in Genesis 21:33—El Olam, or the eternal God. We have allowed liberal theologians to treat the Jews with disrespect—to treat them and their evidence differently from any other evidence found in other cultures elsewhere in history and time. That ought not to be.

The biblical writers held a different worldview than other people; that is why we have a Bible, it's why they are the people of God, and it's why God revealed Himself to them. They are the representatives of the Creator God—the one God who is all-powerful and all-wise. There is only one Yahweh, and the Israelites were chosen to bear His testimony. They did not accept the myths and legends of other peoples, but stood contrary to them and combated their wrong views.

Throughout the ancient Near East, different peoples and cultures produced a variety of creation and Flood stories, but those stories are not uniform in the way that they approach creation or the Flood. Today, we are told the Bible must have borrowed from those cultures because of the fact that the Bible refers to the same events. The assumption is that the biblical writers must have borrowed information from other cultures. Yet we reject that assumption, along with the idea that the Old Testament writers were prescientific.

Debunking the Prescientific Concept

It is a modern fantasy to think that the Israelites believed in a flat earth and a solid-domed sky. The biblical evidence is clear; here are some helpful resources regarding the prescientific discussion. In 1991 Jeffrey Burton Russell published a book titled *Inventing the Flat Earth*, in which he debunks the prescientific concept of the ancient Near East. He suggests that we have imposed this worldview upon them because we think we who live in the modern age are more sophisticated.[2]

In 2006, Noel Weeks, who is from Australia, also wrote a response to a prescientific view of Israel in the *Westminster Theological Journal*, called "Cosmology in Historical Context."[3]

And Jonathan F. Henry addressed the same matter in a 2009 issue of *Journal of Dispensational Theology* with his article "Uniformitarianism in Old Testament Studies."[4]

Dissecting the Creation Account

In Genesis 1:1-25, there is an orderly progression of six days—that is, six literal days of creation. The days are described as having both morning and evening. If these words don't hold their normal, literal meaning, then questions must be raised concerning the significance of each day. However, if "morning" means morning and "evening" means evening, then Genesis 1 speaks of literal days.

In Exodus 20:8-11, a commandment is given to observe the Sabbath, and it is predicated upon the creation account. Because God worked for six days, man must also work six days. If, however, the days in Genesis 1 are actually millions of years, then we must work millions of years for our first day, millions of years for our second day, and so on. Consequently, we would never get to a Sabbath.

As mentioned earlier, the creation has a universal focus. Adam is the head of all mankind, not just the father of Israel. The creation account is theocentric—it is about God, who He is, and how different He is from the views that other cultures have of Him. He is the all-powerful and omniscient Creator who spoke the world into existence. Unlike what certain ancient Near Eastern myths have proclaimed, He did not urinate on some preexisting eternal matter to produce this world. He did not hover and create a cosmic egg out of which we have hatched. Rather, He spoke everything into existence, perfectly preparing the earth for the life that He placed upon it.

Adam and the Image of God

It is important to note that in the creation account, the word "seed" appears 6 times in the first 25 verses—each time in reference to plants. And we are told that plants would produce after their own kind. Then in Genesis 1:26–2:3 we see the first-person plural pronoun used in connection with God: "Then God said, 'Let Us make man in Our image, according to Our likeness'" (1:26). The pronoun must be interpreted as a reference to a plurality within the Godhead—that is, the Trinity. It is not referring to a divine council of the angels, nor is it referring to the popular view of God speaking of Himself in a royal way. Indeed, Paul Joüon, in his Hebrew grammar, emphasizes that there is no such grammatical concept in biblical Hebrew.[5] Rather, this type of statement comes at key points in Scripture and it helps signify the importance of the event that follows. In this case, the emphasis is on man being created in the image of God. No animal is created in the image of God. Nor is mankind created and the image of God inserted at some later point. People were created in the image of God from the very start—"male and female He created them" (Genesis 1:27). In this account we are given the bare outline of what happened. The details come when Moses further elaborates on the event in chapter 2.

Incidentally, Moses used this technique throughout Genesis. He often gave a general description of events—as with the Tower of Babel—then he filled in the details after the broad overview was complete. Genesis chapters 1 and 2 are not two different creation accounts, nor are they two different creations. Notice they are internally consistent if properly read in the light of strict Hebrew grammar. The chronology is not changed, or mistaken—it is the same account, but with a detailed focus on man and how God gives mankind a divine mandate to be fruitful, multiply, and fill the Earth. The ancient reader is thinking at the end of chapter 1, *Well, how are they going to do that?* Genesis 2:4-24 gives the answer, with more information about man and how he is to fulfill the mandate given by God.

The Hebrew word for man is *Adam.* The first time any noun of major importance occurs in the Genesis record, it is usually without the definite article. Thereafter, the article is used as a means of referring back to the first occurrence of the noun. Interestingly, the word *adam*, as a name, does not occur until Genesis 2:20. Adam was naming all of the animals, but no counterpart was found for him. The first time his name is given, it happens in the midst of his naming the animals. Why is this significant? Because God named things when He created them. As part of the divine image that we are given, we have the authority to name things. Adam demonstrates this authority as he names the animals. He also demonstrates the use of language, speech, and reasoning—he is a sophisticated, fully operational human being with highly technical linguistic, mental, and psychological skills. And he exercises the image of God in him when he names the animals.

Notice in Genesis 2:7 that it is clearly a single individual whom God formed out of the dust of the ground. God breathed into this individual's nostrils the breath of life, and Adam became a living being—*one* living being. God placed him into a garden specially prepared for him. In verse 8 we read that "the LORD God planted a garden toward the east, in Eden; and there He placed the man whom He had formed."

We then see in verse 17 that God commanded man not to eat the fruit from the tree of the knowledge of good and evil, and in verse 18 He said that "it is not good for the man to be alone." It is important to remember that this occurs before the end of the sixth day—before Genesis 1:31, when God declares all things to be very good. Part of the reason they are said to be "very good" is because this issue of "not good" was resolved on day six. Why did God say, "It is not good…"? Because man was alone. But Adam cannot be alone if he is a tribe. He is not alone if he is a nation. He is not alone if there are pre-Adamite races. The text tells us that there is only one man. He is alone, and that is not good. God's ultimate design is for him to not be alone. So God searched the animals for an adequate counterpart, and none was found. If Adam were a product of evolution—of animals—you would think that God would have found something suitable for him, but that wasn't so, because none of the animals were made in the image of God.

An adequate counterpart would have to be a bearer of the image of God, just like Adam. Thus God uses Adam's side to produce that counterpart—a woman (2:21-22). This woman then inspires poetry from Adam. The first words that Scripture records from Adam are a poem—a three-lined poem with a triple repetition of "this one." In a climactic fashion, this is the one who is his bone and flesh. This account tells us much about the historicity of Adam. Also, it pushes back on the theory of evolution, for a person who is intelligent and capable enough to produce the sophisticated qualities and cadences of poetry must come from a perfect and omniscient God.

Adam and the Fall

The narrative of Genesis continues as that one man and one woman's story carries on into chapter 3, into the account of the Fall. It is not the fall of a tribe. It is not the fall of a nation. It is the fall of one man. The account is clearly historical, for history is found in the next chapter, with the record of the first murder—the history of Cain and Abel. History is also found in chapter 5 with the generations of Adam to Noah. This account cannot be taken as being mythological; it should be understood as historical and literal. So why would we treat Adam any differently?

Concerning the Fall and the subsequent curse, notice that there is a heritage of real pain, toil, and death. It is not allegorical pain, nor is it figurative toil and death. It is real death, real toil, real pain. There is a literal expulsion of that first man and woman from the garden. Genesis 1:31 affirmed that everything was very good, and then things were not good—they went terribly wrong. But it is not as if God was caught by surprise and had to move to Plan B. God had already set the program of redemption in motion even before He created the earth. He was still following His original plan. That is why we find the mention of a seed in Genesis 3:15. The explanation of the seed here helps to explain how mankind also produces after its kind. The One who is produced as the seed of the woman will have victory over the seed of the serpent.

Also, notice that throughout Genesis 3, the second person singular pronoun is used. That is, God always addresses Adam. This is because, as Paul said, "It was not Adam who was deceived, but the woman" (1 Timothy 2:14). Adam went in with his eyes wide open. He purposely rebelled against God and was accountable for what had occurred. And in the same way that we accept the historicity of Jesus, the promised seed of redemption, we are to accept the historicity of the man who caused the Fall.

Adam and the Canon

Ezekiel 28:13 refers to the Garden of Eden as a historical and literal place. Similarly, Malachi 2:15 looks back and states, "Let no one deal treacherously against the wife of your youth," based upon God's design given in Genesis 2. These are indications that the Genesis record is to be accepted as absolutely true, literal, and historical—not an allegory.

Also, in 1 Chronicles 1:1, we have a genealogy that begins with Adam. The reason that is significant is because in Jesus' day, Chronicles was the last book of the Old Testament. In Luke 11:51-52, when Jesus talked about the murder of God's prophets, He spoke of this as having taken place "from the blood of Abel" (pointing back to Genesis 4) "to the blood of Zechariah" (who was the last prophet recorded in the book of Chronicles—2 Chronicles 24:22). These are the first and the last books of the Old Testament, and Jesus cites them as bookends. So the Old Testament begins and ends with Adam.

The New Testament…can only be built upon a literal historical Adam. It cannot be built on a figurative Adam that is a figment of someone's imagination.

The first book of the New Testament begins with the same terminology: "The record of the genealogy of Jesus the Messiah…" (Matthew 1:1). The writer was carried along by the Holy Spirit to write, in effect, that there is a new Adam, Jesus Christ. And you need to understand the first Adam before you can understand the second Adam. Furthermore, if you read the genealogy in Matthew 1 carefully, it is evident that the word *genesis* occurs several times in the Greek text. It is the same as the title of the book of Genesis—the concept of beginning and birth. Thus the author intentionally ties the Word of God together—the Old Testament begins and ends with Adam, and the New Testament begins and ends with the second Adam in a new heavens and a new earth. It is purposeful, it is designed, and it can only be built upon a literal historical Adam. It cannot be built on a figurative Adam that is a figment of someone's imagination.

Adam and Jesus Christ

In Luke 3:38, the genealogy states that Adam is "the son of God." In other words, he is produced by God. In Romans 5:12, Paul wrote, "Just as through one man sin entered into the world, and death through sin, and so death spread to all men, because all sinned." Paul continued in verse 14, "Nevertheless death reigned from Adam until Moses." Paul then explained the response: "For if by the transgression of the one the many died, much more did the grace of God and the gift by the grace of the one Man, Jesus Christ, abound to the many" (verse 15). Paul was moving through history, from the first Adam to the second Adam. The first Adam brought death; the second Adam brought the response—life.

In like manner, 1 Corinthians 15 refers to the first man and the last man in the context of the historicity of Christ's resurrection. If we deny the legitimacy, historicity, and reality of a literal Adam in 1 Corinthians 15, then we must question the second Adam and His resurrection. And if we do not have a literal and historical resurrection, we of all men are to be most pitied. It is important to note that Paul's message was not in agreement with the rabbis of his day. They had already departed from the truth of God's Word. They were unbelievers who had rejected the Messiah, the prophecies in the Old Testament, and even the literal nature of many of these things—including the existence of Adam as the single historical head of the human race.

The historicity of Adam has a bearing on the historicity of Christ. Thus, the historicity of Adam is a gospel issue. If we deny Adam as a historical man, we must deny Christ's resurrection. If we do that, we destroy the foundations of the Christian faith.

Who Will You Trust?

There is an overemphasis in scholarship today on the similarities between the Bible and ancient Near Eastern materials. However, if we do a comparative analysis, we find out that there are more dissimilarities than there are similarities. Therefore we should not attempt to interpret the Bible in light of ancient Near Eastern material, which affirms polytheism, whereas the Bible affirms monotheism. The ancient Near Eastern texts suggest that physical images were gods, whereas the Bible teaches that idols must be destroyed. The ancient Near Eastern texts have a low view of man, whereas the Scriptures have a high view of man. In the ancient Near

Eastern texts you have conflict and chaos in the creation account; in the Bible, there is no chaos. In the ancient Near Eastern texts there are no uniform standards of ethics; in the Scriptures, there is an expectation of obedience to laws founded upon the character of God.

Despite all of these dissimilarities, it is true that there are certain similarities that exist due to a shared memory of actual events, such as creation and the Flood. God probably explained to Adam how He created everything and why Adam existed. Technically, Adam would be considered the first messenger of God's creation account. And like everything else in a fallen world, that shared memory was skewed by various ancient cultures as they came up with all kinds of myths that relate back to the original creation account.

We must not lift ancient Near Eastern texts above Scripture. Anytime we accept extrabiblical evidence over the biblical record, we denigrate the authority of Scripture.

In sum, there are three possibilities with regard to spiritual authority. One is the authority of the Lord in His written revelation. Another is the authority of the church and its infallible "pope"—not necessarily referring to Catholics, but a teacher, or the chairman of an elder board, or a pastor. A third option is the authority of human reason with its self-styled sovereignty because it does not make sense to understand things the way the Scripture presents them. Which will you choose? Which will you follow as your authority on this issue?

The Word Stands Forever

The Bible requires that we rethink evolution. Methods do not make certain claims true. Scientists are merely interpreters, and the science of origins differs from operational science because it is not possible to reproduce creation in the laboratory. Furthermore, science does not remain the same. Forty years ago, scientists were proclaiming that mountains were formed by isostasy, the accumulation of deposits on the surface on the earth through sedimentation that caused parts of the surface to sink, thereby pushing up other parts and forming mountains. No one believes that today. Rather, it is by the subduction of the tectonic plates that mountains are formed. This change in understanding has occurred in the span of 40 years. That is evidence that science does not remain the same; it changes.

But the word of God is dependable. "The grass withers, the flower fades, but the word of our God stands forever" (Isaiah 40:8). My plea for you is to make God and His Word the authority in determining the historicity of Adam and everything else connected to the creation account.

Why Every Self-Respecting Calvinist Must Be a Six-Day Creationist

"In the beginning God created the heavens and the earth."

Genesis 1:1

4

WHY EVERY SELF-RESPECTING CALVINIST MUST BE A SIX-DAY CREATIONIST

John MacArthur
Shepherds' Conference 2009

Genesis 1–2

Theology was once called the queen of the sciences, which is to say what the Bible taught trumped all other categories, including science. That's a proper title, for the Word of God prompts all other ideas and is absolutely true and accurate. The Bible is not theory, but is instead fact, reality, and truth. The Bible does not take a backseat when it comes to getting things right scientifically, especially when it comes to the creation account.

A God Who Knows

Whoever created the universe and all that is in it understands how it works. Since our God created it, He is not waiting for scientific advances in order to comprehend it. He is not waiting for somebody to discover a system and inform Him about how it works. Since the Creator designed and sustains the universe, He knows the earth is spherical and turns on an axis. He knows it is suspended on nothing, sweeping through space in a fixed rotation in a massive solar system. He knows the staggering riches of the galaxies—the countless stars—and understands black holes better than Stephen Hawking. This Creator knows the cycles of air and water, about chemistry and biology. Whoever is intelligent enough and power-ful enough to design, create, and sustain the incalculable complexity of the universe is certainly intelligent enough to do the relatively simple task of authoring an accurate book that describes it. Therefore, what He tells us will be logically consistent and understandable.

If the Creator had not written a book, no one would know about cre-ation, since only the Creator was there. People could make certain obser-vations and conclusions, but they could never know for sure how it came about.

If the Creator wrote a book about His creation, He would never say the moon is 50,000 leagues higher than the sun and has its own light. He would never say the earth is flat, triangular, and composed of 7 stages, including honey, sugar, butter, and wine; or the earth sits on the heads of countless elephants who produce earthquakes when they shake. That is what the Hindu holy book says—lies that we know were not written by God. The Creator would never say there are only 13 members of the body through which death can come, but that is what the Taoist holy book says. Or that earthquakes are caused by wind moving water, and water moving the land, as the sacred Buddhist source suggests. Or if the Creator of the universe wrote a book, He would not say that Adam fell that men might come into existence and only then they may have joy, as it says in the Book of Mormon.

The true Creator gets it and understands what He has created perfectly. Therefore, when we come to the revelation given to us by the Creator, we are going to get an accurate record.

In the Beginning

With regard to origins, the Bible can be relied on just as it can be trusted with every other subject. Scripture opens with a very simple, clear, and unmistakable statement: "In the beginning God created the heavens and the earth" (Genesis 1:1). God has made it so clear that no one can pos-sibly misunderstand what that means.

In 1903, the English philosopher Herbert Spencer died. He had rejected the Bible, God, and Christ, but was held as a genius because he said there were five categories into which everything that exists can fit:

time, force, action, space, and matter. Yet Scripture already gave the world those categories: "In the beginning"—that's time, "God"—that's force, "created"—that's action, "the heavens"—that's space, "the earth"—that's matter. "In the beginning God created the heavens and the earth" is a profound statement, while at the same time a very simple one. God created, out of nothing, everything that exists—and He did it in six days. Now I want to help you to feel the strength of conviction with regard to the biblical account of creation by hanging some thoughts on three specific words.

Fidelity

The first word we consider is *fidelity*. Simply put, either you believe what Scripture says, or you do not. You can either accept it or reject it, but you cannot alter it. The common response to a statement like that is, "But what about science? Do we not have to apply science to the Genesis account to be intellectually honest?" Christian, get past the idea that you have to have scientific information to understand creation. All science is based on observation, verification, and repetition. Creation had no observers, it cannot be verified as to its means, and it cannot be repeated.

All that creation scientists can do is show that evolution has not happened, and though they can make a good case for that, that doesn't tell us anything about creation itself. One thing we must acknowledge about creation is that it did not happen by any scientific laws; it was a massive miracle. If you deliver yourself from trying to come up with a science of creation, you will be freed from that useless effort. That is why in the Genesis account, and everywhere else in the Bible, we are told repeatedly that God *created*. There are no explicit references, nor are there any implicit references, to any evolutionary process anywhere in the Bible.

There is one historical record of creation in Genesis 1, and then an expansion of the creation of man in Genesis 2. You might say, "Well, do not plants change, develop, and mutate within species?" Of course they do—both plants and animals do. But none of that has anything to do with creation; it does not tell us anything about what happened in six literal days.

For example, let's say you met Lazarus the day after he was raised from the dead. If you were to interview him, you might ask him, "What were you doing when you were away? Where were you? Can I touch your hand?

Can I feel your arm? Can I rub your face? How are you feeling? Do you think the same as you did before you died and were raised? Do you have memories from your past before you were dead?" You could interview him until you are blue in the face, and you could analyze all the processes of his life. You could look at how he eats, how he functions, how he thinks, how he speaks, and how he acts. But that will tell you absolutely nothing about how he came back to life, because that was a supernatural miracle.

When Jesus fed the 5000, you could have taken someone's lunch out of their hand and said, "I'm sorry, but I'm taking this for a scientific experiment. I'm going to analyze the fish and bread, because no one has ever seen fish and bread come out of nowhere." Then after finishing your analysis, let's say you talk to the people and ask them how the food tasted, and whether or not they responded to it the way they do to other food. You could do all that, and it would not tell you anything about how the fish and bread came into existence.

Creation cannot be understood any other way than as a massive miracle revealed by the Creator on the pages of Scripture. Now if you do not believe that, then just say you do not believe it. But do not try to impose upon that massive miracle, which cannot have a scientific explanation, some scientific idea. Doing that is no more helpful than trying to explain how Lazarus came back from the grave by looking at his body. Creation was not a scientific event, and natural law did not play a role, for it was in creation that natural law was created.

Creation is matched only by the future new creation, when God re-creates all things. Neither event is the product of any fixed, repeatable, measurable, or observable scientific laws. All that the reader has is the opportunity to believe or not believe. That is it—fidelity.

You may be thinking, *Well, couldn't God have used evolution?* The question is irrelevant and intrusive, but if you need an answer, no, He could not, because evolution requires death, and there was no death prior to creation and the Fall. Speculation is foolish, and Scripture tells us that God made everything in 6 days. That is either true or not. If it is not true, your problems have just begun, for now you have 66 books with potential errors.

Many people reject the creation account because they do not want

God to be acknowledged—for God is not just the Creator, He is the Law-Giver and the Judge. Evolution was invented in order to eliminate the God of Genesis and obliterate the viability of His moral law. Evolution is the latest means fallen sinners have devised to suppress the innate knowledge of God, to distance themselves from any responsibility to the biblical testimony to which they are accountable, and by which they are either redeemed or condemned.

By embracing evolution, sinners have enthusiastically endeavored to avoid moral responsibility, guilt, and judgment. Evolution is so pointedly hostile to Christianity that it is unthinkable for Christians to embrace it in any way. It is a rejection of biblical revelation. So-called theistic evolution has demonstrated a lack of fidelity to the authority of Scripture, dethroning divine revelation and replacing it with evolutionary theory. Scripture, not science, is the test of everything. Trust in the Scriptures.

Just to give you an illustration, one of the three largest ministries in America claims to be a Bible-based, Christ-proclaiming, and gospel-centered ministry. A letter was sent to the president of this ministry asking their position on origins and Genesis. He responded and said that the ministry takes no stand on origins because it is a "secondary" doctrine. He said that their efforts are designed to bring people together based on the historically essential doctrines of orthodox Christianity, and that creation falls in the category of nonessentials, like eternal security and the rapture. I would suggest that if you want to ask any so-called Christian ministry or church one primary question to determine that ministry's fidelity to the Word of God, ask them this: What is your understanding of Genesis 1?

The answer will reveal their attitude toward Scripture. If they reject Genesis 1 or 2, ask, "At which chapter do you start believing what is said?" Do they kick in at Genesis 3, 6, 9, or maybe Exodus? By the way, you'll want to ask if there are other chapters that they do not believe. How about Isaiah 53? The issue here is not creation; it is fidelity to the Word of God.

Simplicity

The second word to consider is *simplicity*. The Genesis account is, by all honest considerations, very simple, plain, clear, perspicuous, uncomplicated, and unmistakable. There are other accounts of creation outside of Genesis 1: "In the beginning was the Word, and the Word was with God, and the Word was God. He was in the beginning with God. All things came into being through Him, and apart from Him nothing came into being that has come into being" (John 1:1-3). "For by Him all things were created, both in the heavens and on earth, visible and invisible, whether thrones or dominions or rulers or authorities—all things have been created through Him and for Him" (Colossians 1:16).

All biblical references sustain the simple clarity of divine revelation. Take Psalm 104, for example:

> Bless the LORD, O my soul!
>
> O LORD my God, You are very great;
>
> You are clothed with splendor and majesty,
>
> Covering Yourself with light as with a cloak,
>
> Stretching out heaven like a tent curtain.
>
> He lays the beams of His upper chambers in the waters;
>
> He makes the clouds His chariot;
>
> He walks upon the wings of the wind;
>
> He makes the winds His messengers,
>
> Flaming fire His ministers.
>
> He established the earth upon its foundations,
>
> So that it will not totter forever and ever.
>
> You covered it with the deep as with a garment;
>
> The waters were standing above the mountains.
>
> At Your rebuke they fled,
>
> At the sound of Your thunder they hurried away.
>
> The mountains rose; the valleys sank down
>
> To the place which You established for them.
>
> You set a boundary that they may not pass over,
>
> So that they will not return to cover the earth.

He sends forth springs in the valleys;

They flow between the mountains;

They give drink to every beast of the field ;

The wild donkeys quench their thirst.

Beside them the birds of the heavens dwell;

They lift up their voices among the branches.

He waters the mountains from His upper chambers;

The earth is satisfied with the fruit of His works (verses 1-13).

Or Psalm 148:

Praise the LORD!

Praise the LORD from the heavens;

Praise Him in the heights!

Praise Him, all His angels;

Praise Him, all His hosts!

Praise Him, sun and moon;

Praise Him, all stars of light!

Praise Him, highest heavens,

And the waters that are above the heavens!

Let them praise the name of the LORD,

For He commanded and they were created (verses 1-5).

If you deny the creation account, you diminish praise to God. We read in Isaiah 42:5-8:

Thus says God the LORD, who created the heavens and stretched them out, who spread out the earth and its offspring, who gives breath to the people on it and spirit to those who walk in it, "I am the LORD, I have called You in righteousness, I will also hold You by the hand and watch over You, and I will appoint You as a covenant to the people, as a light to the nations, to open blind eyes, to bring out prisoners from the dungeon and those who dwell in darkness from the prison. I am the Lord, that is My name; I will not give My glory to another."

God's creative power in salvation is tied to His power in creation. The worship of God is tied to Him as the Creator. According to the book of Revelation, the God to be worshiped is the one who made the heavens and the earth, and all that is in them. The pattern for worship is God as Creator, and God as the new Creator of those who put their trust in Him.

Also, it is important to note the simple hermeneutic of interpreting Genesis 1–2. If we take everything in Genesis as literal narrative, then why would we consider the first two chapters to be poetic? Genesis is not poetry. There are poetical accounts of creation in the Bible—for example, in Psalm 104 and certain chapters in Job. And they differ completely from the first chapter of Genesis. Ancient Hebrew poetry had certain characteristics, and they are not found in the first chapter of Genesis. So the claim that Genesis 1 is poetry is no solution.

We have fidelity and we have simplicity, and as the church of the Lord Jesus Christ we need to take our stand on the Scriptures at the beginning of the Scriptures. First Timothy 3 teaches that the church of the living God is "the pillar and support of the truth" (verse 15). We are the guardians and the proclaimers of the true God and His true revelation, and that includes the uncomplicated testimony of creation given to us in Genesis.

Priority

The third word for us is *priority*. The creation account is not secondary; it is essential and critical to the main theme of divine revelation and the internal purpose of God. What is God's priority? Why is the universe in existence? Why did God create man? What is the goal, the end, the purpose, the divine priority?

God does not do anything for which He does not have a purpose. The existence of the universe and the theater of the universe must have an ultimate goal. God is achieving something through the countless vast arrays of circumstances, contingencies, changes, and revolutions from person to person and from city to city. God's work does not occur through wild, random minutiae. There is a certain fixed objective to which everyone and everything moves, from creation through providence to consummation.

Jonathan Edwards said it this way: "Providence subordinates all successive changes that come to pass in the state of affairs of mankind."[1] Everything from creation to consummation is part of one great plan being worked out by God's powerful providence. Not one molecule operates outside that plan. History will end, but only when the divine purpose is accomplished—when God's great final goal is achieved. This universe is not eternal; it will end as it began, in a massive display of divine power. It will end, according to 2 Peter 3:10, in an implosion, in which the atoms that make up this universe will melt.

That will happen only when God's scheme is done and He has no further purpose for this universe. Meanwhile, divine providence subordinates, orders, overpowers, and controls all things to achieve that end. We read in Isaiah 46:9, "Remember the former things long past, for I am God, and there is no other; I am God, and there is no one like Me." That is to say there is only one God, so all that exists does so within the purposes of that one God.

We continue reading in Isaiah 46:10 that it is God who declares "the end from the beginning." That is another way of saying, "When I began it, I had already ordained how it would end. From ancient times, I have ordained all that has been happening, saying My purpose will be established, and I will accomplish all My good pleasure." In the end of verse 11 of that same chapter, it is written, "Truly I have spoken; truly I will bring it to pass. I have planned it, surely I will do it." That is a worldview you need to have. For if you reject God as the Creator of all things, you reject the divine purpose that is attached to that creation.

That is why Colossians 1 reminds us that all things were created by Him and for Him. And the grand design is redemption—to gather a bride for His Son, to collect the redeemed. And it will be over when the last person whose name was written in the Lamb's book of life, from before the foundation of the world, is redeemed. All God's work of creation and providence is only a means to achieving the goal of redemption. Every person, every act, every event is subservient to the great purpose of the redemption of sinners. All material realities are subordinated to spiritual objectives. The work of redemption and the work of salvation is God's purpose. The creation of a visible universe and world provides the setting for the creation of an eternal people not yet fully seen.

Paul taught this in Ephesians 3:8-11:

> To me, the very least of all saints, this grace was given, to preach to the Gentiles the unfathomable riches of Christ, and to bring to light what is the administration of the mystery which for ages has been hidden in God who created all things; so that the manifold wisdom of God might now be made known through the church to the rulers and the authorities in the heavenly places. This was in accordance with the eternal purpose which He carried out in Christ Jesus our Lord.

The eternal purpose of God is to redeem a bride for His Son, to take that bride to heaven, and in all of these actions, to display the glory of His grace to the watching holy angels. That great theme is manifested in many ways in the very work of creation.

If you start tampering with Genesis, you start tampering with the understanding of the doctrine of salvation.

We read in 1 Corinthians 15:22, "As in Adam all die, so also in Christ all will be made alive." That is the impact of one man. As there is only one Christ in whom men live, there is only one Adam in whom men die. Romans 5:18 says, "So then as through one transgression there resulted condemnation to all men, even so through one act of righteousness there resulted justification of life to all men." If you start tampering with Genesis, you start tampering with the understanding of the doctrine of salvation. For salvation rests in the one man Christ, just as the doctrine of condemnation rests in the one man Adam.

Not many understand that there are a plethora of salvation analogies that draw from Genesis. One is in 2 Corinthians 4:6: "God, who said, 'Light shall shine out of darkness,' is the One who has shone in our hearts to give the Light of the knowledge of the glory of God in the face of Christ." The analogy is this: Just as God created instantaneous light, so He creates instantaneous spiritual light. This is not some long, drawn-out process. In creation, everything began in a dark and formless void, until God instantly brought light.

Likewise, in salvation, the sinner is in a dark void without form, until the shining glory of God in the face of Jesus Christ enlightens him by a divine miracle. The miracle of spiritual light is analogous to the miracle of physical light. The instantaneous recovery of the elect from the darkness by the power of God—who puts the darkness to flight by opening the heart to gospel light—is a parallel to the darkness that fled at the very words out of God's mouth, "Let there be light." This is not a process; this is a divine miracle.

After that original light was created, more followed in the subsequent days of creation. Jonathan Edwards suggested that this too is a picture of the believer who, though he has been given light and though he has been brought out of the darkness, still experiences the reality of the present darkness. As the creation progresses, there is more beauty and more perfection. It begins with God saying, "This is good." It ends with Him saying, "This is very good." The creation of man on the sixth day is a picture analogous to the creation of the sinner, who is given the light of the glory of God shining in the face of Jesus Christ. In the days after, the sinner moves toward the experience that is more beautiful and more fulfilled, an experience that can be called "very good." If we can keep the analogy going, there is coming a day when this sinner saved by grace will enter into a heavenly rest, where all is light, the eternal Sabbath.

The New Creation

The creation account is also interconnected to the new creation that we as believers are waiting for. It is written in 2 Peter 3:10, "The day of the Lord will come like a thief, in which the heavens will pass away with a roar and the elements will be destroyed with intense heat, and the earth and its works will be burned up." That is Peter's description of the un-creation, of how it all ends. After that there will be a "new heavens and a new earth" (verse 13)—that is, the eternal state—in which righteousness dwells. We have hope that the God who said His creation was "very good" will restore it to that same and even greater status.

Sadly, evangelicals have become more consumed with environmental issues than the future kingdom. *Christianity Today* came out in favor of a recent global warming bill. One evangelical leader said, "The earth is God's body, and He wants us to look after it."[2] In another evangelical's declaration on the care of creation, it was written, "We have sinned in our stewardship of creation; therefore we repent of the way we have polluted, distorted and destroyed the Creator's work."[3] The declaration also said, "We commit ourselves to extend Christ's healing to the creation."[4]

How is it that God is healing the physical earth when He is the one who cursed it? The above-mentioned declaration said, "Human poverty is a consequence of an environmental degradation."[5] Actually, human poverty is a consequence of the failure to subdue the creation by all means necessary. God created everything good, but man sinned and corrupted all of creation. Consequently, the earth has deteriorated from its original goodness and will probably continue to get worse. But it is not because of what man has done to the earth; it is because God cursed it.

If it was not for human care, for using all of our brainpower through the history of mankind to make life good here, this earth would be uninhabitable. You have to use the sweat of your brow to prevent the earth from killing you, but if you subdue it, look at the riches that come out of it. If it weren't for man and his efforts to rule the earth, its riches would never be extracted. The most advanced societies subdue the earth and all its resources for man's benefit. The least-advanced societies, however, live in wastelands of hunger and suffer at the mercy of their environment.

We do not need less energy; we need more. We do not need less technology; we need more. If we want to help the poor, we have got to stop crying about environmentalism, because it only destroys the most deprived people. Many people estimate that global warming efforts will actually kill many people in the next few years, because it halts progress that protects them from the deadly character of the curse. The fact that the scientific community does not rise up and protest the false science means they have been politicized and postmodernized.

The ploy used by postmodern, politicized pseudoscience is what one scientist calls consensus science. That is to say it isn't actually a science, but is a way to shut down real science. The work of science is not done by consensus; science requires only one investigator who is looking for the facts. Consensus is involved only in situations where there is a political, social, and financial agenda, and not scientific support.

A scientist named Bjørn Lomborg wrote a book titled *The Skeptical Environmentalist*. *Scientific American* magazine vilified him as a heretic for even suggesting that anyone had to truly investigate the global warming claims of environmentalists. He does acknowledge that the temperature of the earth has risen, according to some scientists, by one degree in the past 30 years. But 30 years of data is not enough. It is a short-term trend, and trends come and go.

The best information tells us that since 1880, the globe's average temperature has gone up and down. From 1940 to 1970 it was cooler, and from 1970 to the present it has gotten one degree warmer. Legitimate science recognizes a close correlation between sunspots and climate change. The more sunspots, the warmer the climate; so it is solar variations that produce climate change. The sun is the source of temperature changes because of its infrared variations.

There is absolutely no evidence that CO_2 contributes to warming; actually, the opposite is likely true—warming produces more CO_2. The sun warms up the oceans, and when the oceans are warm, they release more CO_2. There is not enough data to determine that a rising temperature globally is produced by people or industry.

Why bring all this up? Because if you let politics, the world, and pseudoscience determine your worldview, then you will be regularly tossed to and fro. Instead, may your fidelity be to the simple and clear Word of God, written for us by the Creator of all things.

We read in the Word that man is not the enemy of nature; he is the steward of it. God gave him this planet to use it. The earth is not a fragile ecosystem that has evolved over billions of years by random chance. It is a strong, robust system held together by God, who upholds all things by His power. This world was never intended to be left pristine; it was intended to be used.

God made the earth. He sustains it, and He tells us that its end will come. May we be ready for that, and may we get our people ready as well by having our focus on nothing but the clear and infallible Word of God.

PRAYER

Father, we thank You for the way You have revealed Yourself. We praise You as the Creator, Sustainer, and Consummator of the universe. The wonder of the staggering reality that You could speak the universe into existence reminds us that You can speak it out of existence just as fast. In the meantime, You sustain it.

Father, only You can tell us the story of creation, and we thank You for doing just that. May we have a renewed commitment to Your Word, to proclaim Your Scripture, to be unequivocal in our devotion and fidelity to that truth. We ask all this in Christ's name. Amen.

Faith of Our Fathers

"The righteous man shall live by faith."

Romans 1:17

5

FAITH OF OUR FATHERS: DO WE HAVE THE SAME GOSPEL AS THE EARLY CHURCH?

Nathan Busenitz

Shepherds' Conference 2012

Selected Scriptures

I t was just over 500 years ago in the fall of 1510 that a desperate Roman Catholic monk made what he thought would be the spiritual pilgrimage of a lifetime. Five years prior to that journey, this man had joined a German monastery, much to the surprise and dismay of his father, who wanted him to become a lawyer.

In fact, it was on his way home from law school that this young man, then 21 years old, found himself in the midst of a severe thunderstorm. The lightning was so intense, he thought for sure he was about to die. Fearing for his life and relying on his Roman Catholic upbringing, he called out for help. "Saint Anne, save me, and I will become a monk!" Fifteen days later, he left law school behind and embraced monastic life; the fear of death had prompted him to become a monk, and the fear of God's wrath would continue to consume him in the years that followed.

He became the most fastidious of all the monks in the monastery, doing everything within his power to placate his guilty conscience and earn God's favor. He dedicated himself to the sacraments, to fasting and penance, he even performed acts of asceticism—like going without sleep, enduring cold winter nights without a blanket, and whipping himself in an attempt to atone for his sins. He would later say about this time in his life that if anyone could have earned heaven by the life of a monk, it would have been him. Even his supervisor, the head of the monastery, became concerned that this young man had grown too introspective and too consumed with questions about his own salvation.

The Righteousness of God

This young monk became particularly fixated on Paul's teachings about the righteousness of God in the book of Romans, especially Romans 1:17, where Paul wrote of the gospel: "In it the righteousness of God is revealed from faith to faith; as it is written, 'But the righteous man shall live by faith.'"

This man's understanding of that verse was clouded. Reading it through the lens of medieval Roman Catholic tradition, he twisted its meaning by thinking that he had to somehow become righteous, through his own efforts, in order to gain salvation. Therein was the problem—he knew he was not righteous. Despite everything he did to try to earn divine favor, he knew he fell short of God's perfect standard.

As he would later recount, he began to hate the phrase "the righteousness of God" because he saw in it his own condemnation. He realized that because God's perfect righteousness was the standard, and because he as a sinner could not meet that standard, then he stood utterly condemned. Out of frustration and despair, he plunged himself even more fervently into the strict practices of monastic life. Trying his best to work his way to salvation, he grew increasingly discouraged.

Hence, it was five years after he became a monk—in the year 1510—that this desperate man made what he thought would be the spiritual pilgrimage of a lifetime. He and a fellow monk traveled in October of that year to the city of Rome. If anyone could help him calm the storm that raged in his soul, he thought, surely it would be the priests, cardinals, and the pope in Rome. Moreover, he was convinced that if he paid homage to the shrines of the apostles and made confession in that holy city, he would secure the greatest absolution possible. He was so excited that when he came within sight of the city, he fell down and exclaimed, "Hail to you, holy Rome, three times holy for the blood of martyrs shed here."[1]

Disappointment in Rome

His excitement soon turned to severe disappointment. He tried to immerse himself in the religious fervor of Rome, visiting the graves of saints, and performing ritualistic acts of penance, but he quickly noticed the glaring inconsistency. As he looked around him—at the pope, the cardinals, and the priests—he did not see righteousness. Instead, he was startled by the corruption, greed, and immorality. The famous historian Philip Schaff explains that the young man was

> …shocked by the unbelief, levity and immorality of the clergy. Money and luxurious living seemed to have replaced apostolic poverty and self-denial. He saw nothing but worldly splendor at the court of Pope Julius II…[and] he heard of the fearful crimes of Pope Alexander VI, which were hardly known and believed in Germany, but freely spoken of as undoubted facts in the fresh remembrance of all Romans…He was told that "if there was a hell, Rome was built on it," and that this state of things must soon end in a collapse.[2]

Here was a desperate man on a desperate journey, having devoted his life to the pursuit of self-righteous legalism. He went to Rome looking for answers, and all he found was spiritual bankruptcy. He returned to Germany disillusioned and disappointed, convinced that "Rome, once the holiest city was now the worst."[3]

A few years after he returned to Germany, Martin Luther would openly defy the pope by calling him the very anti-Christ. He would condemn the cardinals as charlatans, and denounce the apostate tradition of Roman Catholicism for what it had become—a destructive system of works-righteousness. But before that would take place, Luther needed to find the answer to his spiritual dilemma. If he was unrighteous in spite of his best efforts, how could he be made right before a holy and perfect God?

The Heart of the Reformation

In 1513 and 1514, while lecturing through the Psalms and studying the book of Romans, Luther came to realize the glorious truth that had escaped him for so long: The "righteousness of God" not only encompasses the righteous *requirements* of God (of which all men fall short), but also the righteous *provision* of God, whereby He imputes Christ's righteousness to those who repent and believe. Luther's own remarks sum up the glorious transformation that took place in his heart as a result of that discovery. He wrote, "At last, meditating day and night and by the mercy of God…I began to understand that the righteousness of God is that through which the righteous live by a gift of God, namely by faith… Here I felt as if I were entirely born again and had entered paradise itself through the gates that had been flung open."[4]

After a lifetime of guilt—including years of struggling to make himself righteous by trying to please God on his own—Martin Luther finally came to understand the heart of the gospel message. He discovered justification by grace through faith in Christ alone.

For Luther and his fellow Reformers, the doctrine of God's grace became a central part of their preaching and teaching, in direct contradiction to the Roman Catholic doctrine of their day. The five *solas* of the Reformation—*sola Scriptura* ("Scripture alone"), *sola fide* ("faith alone"), *sola gratia* ("grace alone"), *solus Christus* ("Christ alone"), *soli Deo gloria* ("glory to God alone")—summarized the heart and the basis of that Reformation gospel.

"Scripture alone" refers to the fact that God's Word is the church's highest and final authority. "Faith alone" means that justification is not merited on the basis of good works, but is received by "grace alone" through faith in the person and work of Jesus Christ. "Christ alone" emphasizes that the Savior's once-for-all sacrifice at Calvary was perfectly sufficient to pay sin's penalty for those who believe in Him. Consequently, because they can take no credit for their salvation, the redeemed must give all the "glory to God alone."

Did the Reformation Present Something New?

All of this raises a key question: Was Luther's understanding of the gospel something new? In other words, did Martin Luther and the other

Reformers invent the doctrine of justification by grace alone through faith alone based on the finished work of Christ alone?

Some Roman Catholics would certainly argue for that. It was in May of 2007 that Francis Beckwith, then president of the Evangelical Theological Society, announced that he was resigning the position because he was leaving Protestantism to join Roman Catholicism. His reasons were largely related to church history and included statements like, "The early church is more Catholic than Protestant," and Catholics have "more explanatory power to account for both all the biblical texts on justification as well as the church's historical understanding of salvation prior to the Reformation all the way back to the ancient church of the first few centuries."[5]

Another Roman Catholic apologist, with whom I interacted in an online forum, said it this way: "As far as Protestant Christianity goes, it did not exist until the 1500s. I challenge anyone to find the current Protestant beliefs and practices before the 1500s." Later he clarified his point by saying he was looking for someone to show him where Protestant doctrines, such as *sola fide* and *sola Scriptura*, existed before the sixteenth century. He claimed that the evangelical gospel did not exist before the Reformation, and that core Protestant teachings were essentially invented by Martin Luther and the other Reformers. Obviously, that charge would be devastating if it were true.

Reforming Before the Reformation

The fallacious nature of such allegations can be immediately demonstrated by pointing to the pre-Reformers, showing that Luther was actually building on the work of men like John Wycliffe and Jan Hus. Many think of the Reformation as a year in history (1517) or a phenomenon that started with Luther. The reality is that it began to gain momentum as early as the twelfth century. In the 1100s, the Waldensians began to teach that the Bible alone is the authority for the church. They defied papal authority, committed themselves to preaching the Scriptures, and even translated the Word of God into regional dialects so that people could read it in their native language. In the sixteenth century, the Waldensians became part of the Reformation movement because they recognized their doctrinal alignment with the Reformers.

If we move ahead to the 1300s, still two centuries before Martin Luther, we find an English scholar named John Wycliffe, who criticized the corruption of the Catholic system and called for reform. Known as the "Morning Star of the Reformation," Wycliffe (along with fellow scholars at Oxford) translated the Bible into English. A generation later, in the early 1400s, a Bohemian preacher named Jan Hus, having been influenced by both the Waldensians and Wycliffe, opposed the papacy and taught that Christ alone is the head of the church. If Christ is the head of the church, then His Word is the authority in the church—*sola Scriptura*. And if His Word is the authority in the church, then the gospel it presents must be the true message of salvation.

In 1415, after being promised safe passage to the Council of Constance, Hus was arrested, tried, and burned at the stake. A century later, Martin Luther would discover the writings of Jan Hus. He found them so convincing that he became known as the Saxon Hus.

From the Waldensians in the twelfth century, to Wycliffe in the fourteenth, to Hus in the fifteenth, it becomes clear that momentum for the Reformation began to build long before 1517. Luther did not see himself as an innovator, but as someone building on the work of those who had come before him. Nonetheless, this still leaves open the question of the early church: Did believers in the early centuries of church history hold to a gospel of grace alone through faith alone?

The Solas in Scripture

Before answering that question from church history, we must first answer it from the Word of God. As evangelical Christians, Scripture alone is our authority. While we might look to history for affirmation and encouragement, it is not our final authority. Our understanding of the gospel must be established from the clear teaching of the Word of God. The doctrine of justification by grace alone through faith alone must be defended from Scripture, or it cannot be defended at all.

Many passages of Scripture could be cited to make such a defense. For the sake of space, we will reference only a few. In Luke 18:13-14, Jesus contrasted the prayer of a Pharisee with that of a tax collector. He made it clear that we are not justified through our own self-righteous works; rather,

God justifies those who, like the unworthy tax collector, cry out in faith and depend on Him for mercy. Romans 3:28 states that "a man is justified by faith apart from the works of the Law." Romans 4 presents Abraham as an example of that reality, and Romans 5:1 reiterates that because we have "been justified by faith, we have peace with God through our Lord Jesus Christ." In Galatians 3:8, Paul again emphasized "that God would justify the Gentiles by faith." Ephesians 2:8-9 reveals that sinners have been saved by the grace of God, through faith, which is the gift of God and not a result of works.

**We are justified then by His grace alone,
through faith alone, in Christ alone.**

In Philippians 3:8-9, Paul reiterated the bankruptcy of trying to earn salvation on the basis of good works. He explained that he did not have "a righteousness of [his] own derived from the Law, but that which is through faith in Christ, the righteousness which comes from God on the basis of faith." Titus 3:5-7 says God saved us "not on the basis of deeds which we have done in righteousness, but according to His mercy." Later in the text, it states that we are justified by His grace.

Even a brief survey of these passages is sufficient to show that our righteous standing before God is not based on good works that we have done, but only on the finished work of Christ on the cross. We are justified then by His grace alone, through faith alone, in Christ alone.

The First Church Council

What about church history? How did the earliest Christians understand the biblical teaching on justification by faith? There is a place where both biblical truth and church history meet, and it is in the book of Acts. Written by Luke in the early 60s of the first century, the book of Acts includes the first 30 years of the history of the church, starting at Pentecost and ending with Paul's house arrest in Rome.

Acts begins where Luke's Gospel ends, immediately after the resurrection of Jesus Christ. The first chapter centers on the Great Commission, which serves as the outline of the book; Christ's followers were to go
and make disciples in Jerusalem and Judea, Samaria, and the outermost
parts of the earth. We see that mission unfold in Acts. In chapters 2–7,
the church is founded and the gospel spreads throughout Jerusalem and
Judea. In chapter 8, the good news is taken to Samaria. In chapter 9, Saul is
converted; he is the one who will take the gospel to the Gentiles throughout the Roman world. In chapter 10, Luke introduces his readers to the
first Gentile convert, Cornelius. In chapter 11, we have the establishment
of the first Jew-Gentile church in Syrian Antioch. From there to the end
of the book, after a brief note regarding James and Peter in chapter 12, we
read about how Saul (whose Roman name was Paul) takes the gospel to
the Gentile world on several missionary journeys.

The book of Acts celebrates the advancement of the gospel. Yet in the
middle of Luke's historical record (in chapter 15), a serious controversy
arises over the very nature of the gospel itself. The issue was so important
that the apostles met together in Jerusalem to settle the controversy. That
meeting of the apostles is known as the Jerusalem Council—the first council of church history. It met around AD 49 or 50, nearly 20 years after the
church was established on the Day of Pentecost; and 275 years before the
next major church council, the Council of Nicaea.

The Jerusalem Council convened to address one essential question:
"*What is the essence of the gospel?*" Is it a message of grace alone? Or is it a
message of grace plus works? The advancement of the gospel could not
continue unless the right message was being proclaimed.

The Proclamation of the True Gospel (Acts 13–14)

At the outset of church history, starting with the day of Pentecost (Acts
2), the church was composed entirely of Jewish Christians. It wasn't until
the conversion of the Samaritans (in Acts 8) and Cornelius (in Acts 10)
that non-Jews began to be incorporated into the body of Christ. After
highlighting Cornelius's conversion, Luke detailed the spread of the gospel into Gentile lands (in Acts 11:19–24), culminating in the formation of
a predominantly Gentile church in Syrian Antioch.

The inclusion of Gentiles into the church represented a major paradigm shift for Jewish Christians. For the previous 1500 years, since the time of Moses, God had been working through the nation of Israel. But now, in the church, Gentiles were being saved without having to first become Jewish proselytes. Of course, God had prepared the apostles for this by saving Cornelius while Peter was present (Acts 11:1-18). So when the apostles heard about Gentile converts in Antioch, they rejoiced and sent Barnabas to pastor the believers there. A short time later, Barnabas went to Tarsus, found Paul, and brought him back to serve alongside of him in Antioch (Acts 11:25-26).

After a season of fruitful ministry, around the year AD 47, Paul and Barnabas embarked on an evangelistic mission to several Gentile cities in Southern Galatia, in modern-day Turkey. They travelled first to Cyprus, then to Perga, and then to Psidian Antioch. It was there, in Antioch, that they entered the synagogue and Paul preached a powerful gospel message to the Jewish people in attendance.

The content of that sermon is recorded in Acts 13:16-41, and it centered on the fact that Jesus is the Messiah whom God raised from the dead so that sinners might be saved through Him. In his emphasis on the gospel of grace, Paul declared in verses 38-39: "Therefore let it be known to you, brethren, that through this Man [Jesus Christ] is preached to you the forgiveness of sins; and by Him everyone who believes is justified from all things from which you could not be justified by the law of Moses" (NKJV).

In contrast to the popular self-righteous legalism of first-century Judaism, Paul asserted that faith in Christ can do what keeping the law of Moses could never do. Forgiveness and justification come only through believing in Christ, and not through keeping the works of the Law. That would have been a revolutionary concept for those who heard Paul preach in the synagogue that day. Not surprisingly, many of them rejected it (verses 45-46), forcing Paul and Barnabas to leave the city (verse 50).

In Acts 14:27-28, Paul and Barnabas finally returned home, after preaching the gospel in several other cities, establishing churches, and appointing leaders in those congregations. Their first missionary journey was over, and it had been a great success. Though it had lasted many months, and though Paul and Barnabas were severely persecuted and nearly killed, churches had been planted throughout southern Galatia. The gospel of faith alone had been proclaimed to the Gentiles. But controversy was about to erupt.

The Perversion of the True Gospel (Acts 15:1-5)

Acts 14 ends with the church in Syrian Antioch rejoicing over the success of the first missionary journey. By contrast, Acts 15 opens with these words:

> Some men came down from Judea and began teaching the brethren, "Unless you are circumcised according to the custom of Moses, you cannot be saved." And when Paul and Barnabas had great dissension and debate with them, the brethren determined that Paul and Barnabas and some others of them should go up to Jerusalem to the apostles and elders concerning this issue. Therefore, being sent on their way by the church, they were passing through both Phoenicia and Samaria, describing in detail the conversion of the Gentiles, and were bringing great joy to all the brethren. When they arrived at Jerusalem, they were received by the church and the apostles and the elders, and they reported all that God had done with them. But some of the sect of the Pharisees who had believed stood up, saying, "It is necessary to circumcise them and to direct them to observe the Law of Moses" (verses 1-5).

On the heels of a successful missionary venture, the church suddenly found itself embroiled in controversy over the essential nature of the gospel. The fundamental issue could be summed up with this question: What must sinners do to be saved? (cf. Acts 16:30).

In Acts 13:38-39, Paul declared that faith in Christ does what the Law of Moses could not do: It brings both forgiveness and justification. But these former Pharisees, who later became known as the Judaizers, claimed that the gospel Paul had been preaching was illegitimate unless it also incorporated works. In addition to faith, they argued that both circumcision (Acts 15:1-2) and keeping the Mosaic Law (Acts 15:5) were necessary for salvation. It is no wonder that great dissension and debate arose among them, for this was no small matter. To settle the matter, Paul and Barnabas traveled to Jerusalem to consult with the apostles and elders there. Is salvation by grace alone, or is it by faith plus circumcision and the works of the Mosaic Law?

You might be wondering what Paul was thinking when he came to the Jerusalem Council. He tells us in the second chapter of Galatians, a letter which he wrote shortly after these events. Paul wrote, "I went up again to Jerusalem with Barnabas, taking Titus along also. It was because of a revelation that I went up; and I submitted to them the gospel which I preach among the Gentiles, but I did so in private to those who were of reputation, for fear that I might be running, or had run, in vain" (Galatians 2:1-2).

Paul came to Jerusalem and, before the council convened publicly, met with some of the apostolic leaders privately, explaining to them the gospel he had been preaching to the Gentiles—the gospel of grace alone through faith alone. The passage identifies these leaders as James, the brother of the Lord, Peter, and John. Notice what Paul said about the Judaizers in Galatians 2:4-5: "It was because of the false brethren secretly brought in, who had sneaked in to spy out our liberty which we have in Christ Jesus, in order to bring us into bondage. But we did not yield in subjection to them for even an hour, so that the truth of the gospel would remain with you." As those words make clear, Paul was determined not to compromise on the truth of the gospel.

The Preservation of the True Gospel (Acts 15:6-11)

After Paul met with these apostolic leaders privately, the public council took place. Luke describes the scene, starting in verse 6:

> The apostles and the elders came together to look into this matter. After there had been much debate, Peter stood up and said to them, "Brethren, you know that in the early days God made a choice among you, that by my mouth the Gentiles would hear the word of the gospel and believe. And God, who knows the heart, testified to them giving them the Holy Spirit, just as He also did to us; and He made no distinction between us and them, cleansing their hearts by faith. Now therefore why do

you put God to the test by placing upon the neck of the disciples a yoke which neither our fathers nor we have been able to
bear? But we believe that we are saved through the grace of the
Lord Jesus, in the same way as they also are."

Notice that Peter affirmed that it was right for the Gentiles to hear the
gospel and believe. In verse 8, he confirmed that the Gentiles had received
the Holy Spirit just as the Jewish believers had on the day of Pentecost.
In verse 9, he emphasized that God had cleansed their hearts by faith. In
verse 10, he stated that the Mosaic Law was a burden that was not necessary for salvation. And in verse 11, he reiterated that all believers, both Jew
and Gentile, are saved by the grace of the Lord. This was a clear affirmation
by Peter of the gospel of grace, apart from the works of the law, through
faith in Christ alone.

Verses 12 and following indicate that James and the rest of the Jerusalem Council agreed with Peter, noting that Gentile Christians did not
need to keep the Mosaic Law.[6] The gospel preached by Paul and Barnabas was wholeheartedly affirmed by the apostles at the Jerusalem Council as being the true gospel. Consequently, Paul and Barnabas returned to
Antioch greatly encouraged and filled with joy (Acts 15:30-31).

In spite of the council's clear decision, the Judaizers would continue to
cause problems. In the very churches Paul and Barnabas planted on their
first missionary journey, false teachers began to insist that faith alone was
insufficient for salvation. Instead, they claimed that circumcision and law-
keeping were required for Gentile believers to be saved. One can imagine
how concerned Paul would have been.

He responded in two ways: by planning a follow-up visit to those
churches (Acts 15:36), and by sending them a letter, in which he offered
them a stern warning:

> I am amazed that you are so quickly deserting Him who called
> you by the grace of Christ, for a different gospel; which is really
> not another; only there are some who are disturbing you and
> want to distort the gospel of Christ. But even if we, or an angel
> from heaven, should preach to you a gospel contrary to what
> we have preached to you, he is to be accursed! As we have said

before, so I say again now, if any man is preaching to you a gospel contrary to what you received, he is to be accursed! (Galatians 1:6-9).

The apostle went on to clearly explain that justification is not based on doing the works of the law, but is only granted by grace through faith in Christ (cf. Galatians 3:1-14). That theme continued to be a primary emphasis throughout Paul's writings over the course of his entire ministry (cf. Romans 4–5; Ephesians 2:8-9; Philippians 3:7-11; Titus 3:4-7).

The biblical truth that salvation is only by grace, and not by our own efforts, is what liberated Luther and his fellow Reformers from the system of works righteousness in which they had been trapped. But what about the early leaders of Christianity who lived in the centuries after the apostles? Did they also understand justification to be by grace alone through faith alone in Christ alone?

The Church Fathers

Evangelicals rightly conclude that the Reformation doctrine of *sola fide* is grounded in Scripture. But many wrongly assume that such an understanding of the gospel is absent from pre-Reformation church history. In reality, glimpses of "grace alone" and "faith alone" can be found throughout the writings of both the church fathers and a number of medieval theologians. A full survey would demand a book-length treatment.[7] However, a brief list is sufficient to illustrate the point.

Clement of Rome (d. ca. 100)

Clement of Rome was the pastor of the church in Rome from about AD 90 to 100. As a church leader, he was a contemporary of the apostle John. He was likely a disciple of Paul, and may even be the Clement mentioned in Philippians 4:3.

The Roman Catholic Church considers Clement to be a pope, which makes his affirmation of *sola fide* all the more significant. His epistle to the Corinthians is likely the earliest Christian document that we have outside of the New Testament. In chapter 32 of his letter, he says of believers:

And so we, having been called through his will in Christ Jesus, are not justified through ourselves or through our own wisdom or understanding or piety, or works that we have done in holiness of heart, but through faith, by which the Almighty God has justified all who have existed from the beginning; to whom be the glory for ever and ever. Amen.[8]

Clement clearly understood justification to be received by faith apart from any meritorious acts on the part of the believer. Though he does not use the word "alone," he excludes any category that might be added to saving faith ("ourselves," "our own wisdom or understanding or piety," "works that we have done in holiness of heart"). These categories cannot justify, because sinners are justified by grace through faith, apart from any works.

To Clement's testimony, a chorus of other voices might be added:

Polycarp (ca. 69–155)

Polycarp pastored the church in Smyrna in the first half of the second century. His faithfulness, even in the face of death, is famously recorded in *The Martyrdom of Polycarp*. In his *Epistle to the Philippians*, his only surviving letter, Polycarp echoes the truth of Ephesians 2:8-9 when he writes:

I also rejoice because your firmly rooted faith, renowned from the earliest times, still perseveres and bears fruit to our Lord Jesus Christ, who endured for our sins, facing even death, whom God raised up, having loosed the birth pangs of Hades. Though you have not seen him, you believe in him with an inexpressible and glorious joy (which many desire to experience), knowing that by grace you have been saved, not because of works, but by the will of God through Jesus Christ.[9]

As Polycarp articulates, salvation is a gift of God's grace and cannot be earned on the basis of good works.

The Epistle to Diognetus (second century)

This anonymous epistle is an early evangelistic tract written to an unbeliever. Its beautiful presentation of the gospel makes it one of the most eloquent works of patristic literature. Notice the author's clear understanding of Christ's imputed righteousness given to those who embrace Him in saving faith:

> He gave His own Son as a ransom for us, the holy One for transgressors, the blameless One for the wicked, the righteous One for the unrighteous, the incorruptible One for the corruptible, the immortal One for them that are mortal. For what other thing was capable of covering our sins than His righteousness? By what other one was it possible that we, the wicked and ungodly, could be justified, than by the only Son of God? O sweet exchange! O unsearchable operation! O benefits surpassing all expectation! That the wickedness of many should be hid in a single righteous One, and that the righteousness of One should justify many transgressors![10]

Fourteen centuries later, Martin Luther would similarly celebrate the great exchange that takes place at the moment of salvation.[11] Christ bore the sins of believers on the cross so that they might be clothed in His perfect righteousness (2 Corinthians 5:21).

Hilary of Poitiers (ca. 300–368)

In the fourth century, Hilary of Poitiers wrote a commentary on the Gospel of Matthew. Significantly, he included the phrase "faith justifies" or "we are justified by faith" more than 20 times in that work. For example, he writes, "Wages cannot be considered as a gift, because they are due to work, but God has given free grace to all men by the justification of faith."[12] Commenting on the hostility of the Pharisees, he remarks, "It disturbed the scribes that sin was forgiven by a man (for they considered that Jesus Christ was only a man) and that sin was forgiven by Him whereas the Law was not able to absolve it, since faith alone justifies."[13] These, and similar statements, indicate that Hilary understood that justification is received through faith, apart from works.

Basil of Caesarea (329–379)

In his *Sermon on Humility*, Basil of Caesarea explains why believers can take no credit for their salvation:

This is perfect and pure boasting in God, when one is not proud on account of his own righteousness but knows that he is indeed unworthy of the true righteousness and is justified solely by faith in Christ. And Paul boasts that he despises his own righteousness, seeking that righteousness that is on account of Christ, which is the righteousness of God by faith.[14]

Following Paul's lead in Philippians 3:1-11, Basil reiterates that believers are "justified solely by faith in Christ." Such an affirmation of faith alone (*sola fide*) motivates Basil to boast only in God for his salvation (*soli Deo gloria*).

Ambrosiaster (fourth century)

The fourth-century Pauline commentator known as Ambrosiaster makes numerous statements affirming justification by grace through faith in his commentary on Romans. Here are three brief examples:

They are justified freely because, while doing nothing or providing any repayment, they are justified by faith alone as a gift of God.[15]

Paul tells those who live under the law that they have no reason to boast basing themselves on the law and claiming to be of the race of Abraham, seeing that no one is justified before God except by faith.[16]

Those are blessed of whom God has decreed that, without work or any keeping of the law, they are justified before God by faith alone.[17]

John Chrysostom (347–407)

The renowned fourth-century preacher John Chrysostom expresses the truth of justification by grace through faith alone on many occasions in his *Homilies*. Here is a small handful of examples:

What is the "law of faith"? It is, being saved by grace. Here he shows God's power, in that He has not only saved, but has even justified, and led them to boasting, and this too without needing works, but looking for faith only.[18]

Would you know how good our Master is? The Publican went up full of ten thousand wickednesses, and saying only, "Be merciful unto me," went down justified.[19]

Attend to this point. He Himself who gave the Law, had decreed, before He gave it, that the heathen should be justified by faith…They said that he who kept not the Law was cursed, but he proves that he who kept it was cursed, and he who kept it not, blessed. Again, they said that he who adhered to faith alone was cursed, but he shows that he who adhered to faith alone, is blessed.[20]

For the Law requires not only faith but works also, but grace saves and justifies by faith.[21]

For as people, on receiving some great good, ask themselves if it is not a dream, as not believing it; so it is with respect to the gifts of God. What then was it that was thought incredible? That those who were enemies and sinners, justified by neither the law nor works, should immediately through faith alone be advanced to the highest favor. On this head [topic] accordingly Paul has discoursed at length in his Epistle to the Romans, and here again at length. "This is a faithful saying," he says, "and worthy of all acceptation, that Christ Jesus came into the world to save sinners." As the Jews were chiefly attracted by this, he persuades them not to listen to the law, since they could not attain salvation by it without faith. Against this he contends, for it seemed to them incredible that a person who had misspent all his former life in vain and wicked actions should afterwards be saved by his faith alone. On this account he says, "It is a saying to be believed."[22]

[God] has justified our race not by right actions, not by toils, not by barter and exchange, but by grace alone. Paul, too, made this clear when he said: "But now the justice of God has been made manifest apart from the Law." But the justice [or, righteousness] of God comes through faith in Jesus Christ and not through any labor and suffering.[23]

Marius Victorinus (fourth century)

In his commentary on Ephesians, Marius Victorinus writes, "[God] did not give back to us what was merited, since we did not receive this by merits but by the grace and goodness of God."[24] Later he adds, "The fact that you Ephesians are saved is not something that comes from yourselves. It is the gift of God. It is not from your works, but it is God's grace and God's gift, not from anything you have deserved."[25] And again, "Only faith in Christ is salvation for us."[26] Elsewhere, commenting on Galatians, he looks to the example of Abraham as the archetype of justification by faith:

> For the patriarchs prefigured and foretold that man would be justified from faith. Therefore, just as it was reckoned as righteousness to Abraham that he had faith, so we too, if we have faith in Christ and every mystery of his, will be sons of Abraham. Our whole life will be accounted as righteous.[27]

Augustine (354–430)

Augustine was the most influential church father, at least in the West. Accordingly, his emphasis on God's grace in salvation significantly influenced the thinking of the Reformers. That emphasis is clearly seen in excerpts from Augustine's writings. Consider the following:

> When someone believes in him who justifies the impious, that faith is reckoned as justice to the believer, as David too declares that person blessed whom God has accepted and endowed with righteousness, independently of any righteous actions. What righteousness is this? The righteousness of faith, preceded by no good works, but with good works as its consequence.[28]

> What is grace? That which is freely given. What is "freely given"? Given, not paid. If it was due, wages would be given, but grace would not be bestowed. But if it was really due, then you were

good. But if, as is true, you were evil but believed on him who justifies the ungodly. (What is, "who justifies the ungodly"? the ungodly is made righteous), consider what by right hung over you by the law and you have obtained by grace. But having obtained that grace by faith, you will be just by faith—"for the just lives by faith."[29]

Now, having duly considered and weighed all these circumstances and testimonies, we conclude that a man is not justified by the precepts of a holy life, but by faith in Jesus Christ; in a word, not by the law of works, but by the law of faith; not by the letter, but by the spirit; not by the merits of deeds, but by free grace.[30]

Prosper of Aquitaine (390–455)

An early defender and systematizer of Augustinian doctrine was Prosper of Aquitaine. Following Augustine's emphasis on grace, Prosper declared:

Just as there are no crimes so detestable that they can prevent the gift of grace, so too there can be no works so eminent that they are owed in condign [deserved] judgment that which is given freely. Would it not be a debasement of redemption in Christ's blood [literally, would not the redemption of Christ's blood become valueless], and would not God's mercy be made secondary to human works, if justification, which is through grace, were owed in view of preceding merits, so that it were not the gift of a Donor, but the wages of a laborer?[31]

As Prosper explains, no crimes are so egregious that they are beyond the reach of God's grace. Conversely, no good works are so noble that they can merit salvation. The gift of salvation is given freely, which means it cannot be earned on the basis of works. To think that it can is a debasement of Christ's sacrifice on the cross.

Theodoret of Cyrrhus (ca. 393–457)

Theodoret of Cyrrhus expresses a similar understanding of salvation by grace through faith apart from works. In his commentary on Romans, he states, "The doer of righteousness expects a reward, but justification by faith is the gift of the God of all."[32] Earlier in that same work, he writes:

> The righteousness of God is not revealed to everyone but only to those with the eyes of faith. For the holy apostle teaches us that God foresaw [literally, planned] this for us from the beginning and predicted it through the prophets, and even before the prophets, had it hidden in his secret will…Paul quoted Habakkuk for the benefit of the Jews, because he wanted to teach them not to cling to the provisions of the law but to follow [their own] prophets. For many centuries before they had predicted that one day there would be salvation by faith alone.[33]

Theodoret's commentary on Ephesians evidences a similar perspective. Speaking of Christ, he explains,

> Since He rose we hope that we too shall rise. He Himself [by His rising] has paid our debt. Then Paul explains more plainly how great the gift is: "You are saved by grace." For it is not because of the excellence of our lives that we have been called, but because of the love of our Savior.[34]

Again he writes,

> All we bring to grace is our faith. But even in this faith, divine grace itself has become our enabler. For [Paul] adds, "And this is not of yourselves but it is a gift of God; not of works, lest anyone should boast" (Eph. 2:8-9). It is not of our own accord that we have believed, but we have come to belief after having been called; and even when we had come to believe, He did not require of us purity of life, but approving mere faith, God bestowed on us forgiveness of sins.[35]

Accordingly, Theodoret can use the language of *faith alone* to describe the hope of salvation: "I consider myself wretched—in fact, wretched three times over. I am guilty of all kinds of errors. Through faith alone I look for finding some mercy in the day of the Lord's appearing."[36]

Anselm of Canterbury (1033–1109)

If we jump ahead to the medieval period, we still find glimpses of the gospel of grace through faith apart from works. For example, in his *Exhortation to a Dying Man*, Anselm of Canterbury instructed those on the verge of death to trust only in Christ for their salvation, and not in their own merits. He articulated this truth in the form of a question: "Do you hope and believe, that not by your own merits, but by the merits of the passion [death] of Jesus Christ, you may attain to everlasting salvation?" He then instructed his readers to respond by saying, "I do." In that same context, he wrote:

> Come then, while life remains in you, in His death alone place your whole trust; in nothing else place any trust; to His death commit yourself wholly; with this alone cover yourself wholly; in this enwrap yourself wholly. And if the Lord your God wishes to judge you, say, "Lord, between Your judgment and me I present the death of our Lord Jesus Christ; in no other way can I contend with You." And if He says that you are a sinner; say, "Lord, I interpose the death of our Lord Jesus Christ between my sins and You." If He says that you have deserved condemnation; say, "Lord, I set the death of our Lord Jesus Christ between my evil deserts and You; and His merits I offer for those which I ought to have, but have not." If He says that He is angry with you; say, "Lord I set the death of our Lord Jesus Christ between Your wrath and me." And when you have completed this, say again, "Lord, I set the death of our Lord Jesus Christ between You and me."[37]

Bernard of Clairvaux (1090–1153)

A final example comes from Bernard of Clairvaux. Four centuries later, Martin Luther and his fellow Reformers would be deeply impacted by Bernard's teaching on justification by grace through faith alone. Here are a few citations that demonstrate why the Reformers were drawn to Bernard. He writes:

> For what could man, the slave of sin, fast bound by the devil, do of himself to recover that righteousness which he had

formerly lost? Therefore he who lacked righteousness had another's imputed to him…It was man who owed the debt, it was man who paid it. For if one, says [the apostle Paul], died for all, then all were dead, so that, as One bore the sins of all, the satisfaction of One is imputed to all. It is not that one forfeited, another satisfied; the Head and body is one, viz., Christ. The Head, therefore, satisfied for the members, Christ for His children.[38]

I confess myself most unworthy of the glory of heaven, and that I can never obtain it by my own merits. But my Lord possesses it upon a double title: that of natural inheritance, by being the only begotten Son of his eternal Father; and that of purchase, he having bought it with his precious blood. This second title he has conferred on me; and, upon this right, I hope with an assured confidence, to obtain it through his praiseworthy passion and mercy.[39]

As for your justice, so great is the fragrance it diffuses that you are called not only just but even justice itself, the justice that makes men just. Your power to make men just is measured by your generosity in forgiving. Therefore the man who through sorrow for sin hungers and thirsts for justice, let him trust in the One who changes the sinner into a just man, and judged righteous in terms of faith alone, he will have peace with God.[40]

It is hard to imagine a better summary of the Reformation doctrine of *sola fide* than that final line—namely, that sinners are "judged righteous in terms of faith alone" and therefore they "have peace with God."

How We Got Here

As the above survey demonstrates, the claim that the doctrine of *sola fide* is without historical warrant is, itself, without warrant. That sinners are justified by grace through faith alone was not a Reformation invention. It was the clear teaching of the apostles in the New Testament, and echoes of that truth can be traced throughout church history.

But how did this message get lost in history, such that the Reformation was necessary? The answer to that question is complex—because the shift took place gradually over centuries of time, as manmade traditions began to obscure the purity of the gospel.

The medieval Catholic Church eventually came to define justification in synergistic terms (meaning that the church presented salvation as a cooperative effort between God and man). In the thirteenth century, at the Fourth Lateran Council (1215), the Roman Catholic Church officially made salvation contingent on good works by establishing the seven sacraments as the means by which sinners are justified.

As Norm Geisler and Josh Betancourt explain in their book *Is Rome the True Church?*:

> Roman Catholicism as it is known today is not the same as the Catholic Church before 1215. Even though the split between East and West occurred in 1054, most non-Catholics today would have been able to belong to the Catholic Church before the thirteenth century. Regardless of certain things the church permitted, none of its official doctrinal proclamations regarding essential salvation doctrines were contrary to orthodoxy.

> While the development of Roman Catholicism from the original church was gradual, beginning in early centuries, one of the most significant turning points came in 1215, when one can see the beginning of Roman Catholicism as it is subsequently known. It is here that the seeds of what distinguishes Roman Catholicism were first pronounced as dogma. It is here that they pronounced the doctrine of transubstantiation, the primacy of the bishop of Rome, and seven sacraments. Many consider this a key turning point in the development of Roman Catholicism in distinction from non-Catholic forms of Christianity.[41]

Thomas Aquinas (1225–1274), who was born ten years after the Fourth Lateran Council, also contributed greatly to confusion on the true nature of the gospel. As Gregg R. Allison explains:

> More than anyone else, Thomas Aquinas set down the medieval Catholic notion of justification and its corollaries of grace,

human effort, and merit. Although a substantial departure from Augustine and the Augustinians of the Middle Ages, his theology became determinative for the Roman Catholic Church…[Thomas] emphasized the grace of God yet prescribed an important role for human cooperation in obtaining salvation. Certainly, God exercises the primary role in achieving and applying salvation, but people have their part to play as well. God moves by initiating grace in a person's life; then that person moves toward God and moves away from sin, resulting in the forgiveness of sins. Thus, Aquinas believed in a synergy, or cooperative effort, between God and people in justification.[42]

To base salvation on a cooperative effort between God's grace *and* our good works presents a major problem, for it distorts the biblical teaching about grace. As Paul explained about salvation, "If it is by grace, it is no longer on the basis of works, otherwise grace is no longer grace" (Romans 11:6). To add works into the equation is to frustrate grace. Certainly, good works are the *fruit* of salvation, but they are not the *foundation* of it. And it was at that point that medieval Catholicism muddled up the gospel.

By the thirteenth century, then, the official doctrines of the Roman Catholic Church had become fully corrupt, which brings us back full circle to the pre-Reformers. By the middle of the twelfth century, the Waldensians were questioning certain errors they saw in the Roman Catholic system. In the fourteenth century, John Wycliffe; in the fifteenth century, Jan Hus; and then in the sixteenth century, Martin Luther saw these errors as well.

Importantly, the Reformers saw their teachings as the *recovery* of truth that was very old, not the *invention* of something new. They looked to Scripture as the authoritative basis for doctrine, but they also studied the church fathers—contending that their teachings were in line with historic orthodoxy. John Calvin explained the Reformers' perspective on the church fathers with these words, "[The Roman church] unjustly set the ancient fathers against us (I mean the ancient writers of a better age of the church) as if in them, they had supporters of their own impiety…But we do not despise them [the church fathers]; in fact, if it were to our present purpose, I could with no trouble at all prove that the greater part of what we are saying today meets their approval."[43]

Rather than rejecting the early church's understanding of the gospel, the Reformers worked tirelessly to recover the very gospel championed and cherished by the apostles and those who lived in the centuries after them. That reality should be encouraging for those of us who preach, believe, and love that same gospel today.

Mastering the Doctrine of Justification

"If we, or an angel from heaven, should preach to you
a gospel contrary to what we have preached to you,
he is to be accursed."

Galatians 1:8

6

MASTERING THE DOCTRINE
OF JUSTIFICATION

R.C. Sproul
Shepherds' Conference 2005

Galatians 1:6-10

There is no place in the entire corpus of the apostle Paul where he speaks as strongly as he does in Galatians 1 to those who are moving away from the purity of the gospel. The apostle Paul expressed his astonishment to the Galatians, saying,

> I am amazed that you are so quickly deserting Him who called you by the grace of Christ, for a different gospel; which is really not another; only there are some who are disturbing you and want to distort the gospel of Christ. But even if we, or an angel from heaven, should preach to you a gospel contrary to what we have preached to you, he is to be accursed (Galatians 1:6-8).

Paul went on to write, "For am I now seeking the favor of men, or of God? Or am I striving to please men? If I were still trying to please men, I would not be a bond-servant of Christ" (verse 10). The last thought Paul attached to the warning of departing from the gospel is that of pleasing human beings. The apostle learned early in his ministry that to please men can be to displease Christ—a reminder that we need every day as we seek to serve Him with faithfulness and preach the true gospel.

A Few Introductory Questions

I would like to ask three questions: First, how many of you are Protestants? Second, how many of you are evangelicals? Third, how many of you have been ordained or are otherwise serving in some capacity in what we call the gospel ministry?

If you have answered yes to any of those, then here are a few follow-up questions: If you are Protestant, what are you protesting? If you are an evangelical, how has that term been defined historically? And if you have been separated unto ministry, what is the gospel to which you are testifying?

I ask those questions because I am assuming that the vast majority of people who define themselves as Protestants have no idea what they are protesting. Also, there is a real crisis in our day about the very meaning of the term *evangelical*. Historically it described those who, in the Protestant Reformation, rediscovered the *evangel*, which is Latin for the gospel. Since the sixteenth century, there has been no period of time within Protestantism that the doctrine of justification by faith alone, which is at the heart of the *evangel*, has been more deeply obscured among professing evangelicals than it is today.

Presently, there are people who call themselves evangelical while at the same time denying the historic and biblical doctrine of justification by faith alone. This occurs so often that we can no longer just use the term *evangelical* to describe where we stand theologically. Most concerning to me is the loss of the understanding as to what comprises the substance of the gospel.

For example, I was at a meeting in Washington a few years ago where some of the leading so-called evangelical representatives of the world had gathered. One leader in particular was asked by the press, "What is the gospel?" This man, whose name I will not reveal to protect the guilty, was quiet for a while, and then he said, "It means the good news that Jesus can change your life, and you can have a personal relationship with Him." He stumbled around for a few more minutes, but it was absolutely clear the man did not have a clue as to the meaning of the gospel in biblical terms. I am greatly concerned about that, which is why I am going to look with you at the doctrine of justification by faith alone.

Painting a Caricature

I intend to proceed with an overview of the Roman Catholic doctrine of justification because I have found that teaching from this pedagogical perspective helps the student grasp the biblical doctrine of justification. It is extremely beneficial to teach this truth against the backdrop of what the controversy was about during the Reformation in the sixteenth century.

The second reason I always begin with the Roman Catholic view of justification when I teach this doctrine is because it has been my experience that the vast majority of pastors with whom I speak about the classic controversy with Rome have very little understanding of the Roman Catholic view of justification. They have bought into the myth that Rome has recently changed from its sixteenth-century version of itself. There is the idea abounding that Rome has altered its doctrine of justification and now embraces what Luther was trying to get her to embrace. Nothing, of course, can be further from the truth. Although Rome has changed with respect to certain things since the sixteenth century, there are far more problems to resolve today.

One reason that misperception permeates contemporary evangelicalism is because professing evangelicals do not know the Roman Catholic view. Part of that is because we have, in many cases, slandered the Roman Catholic community by vastly oversimplifying the difference between us and them, and by telling everybody that Rome believes we are justified by works, not by faith; by merit, not by grace; by ourselves, and not by Christ. Yet this is a terrible slander because the Roman Catholic Church in the sixteenth century, the twentieth century, and the twenty-first century has insisted and continues to insist that there is no justification apart from grace, no justification apart from faith, and no justification apart from Christ.

What we usually do is set up a caricature of the Roman doctrine of justification by describing what is actually classic Pelagianism, which the Roman Church repudiated early on and once again at the Council of Trent in the sixteenth century. In every official occasion that Rome has addressed this issue, she has categorically repudiated pure Pelagianism, which says that a person can get to heaven without grace, without Christ, without faith, and simply by living a good life. If we are to be clear in our understanding of justification, we have to understand what Rome does teach as well as what she does not teach.

Consistent Through the Years

During the Year of Jubilee, Catholic popes will open what's known as the Holy Door, through which people can come to visit the pope and get a plenary indulgence. This event occurs every 50 years in the Roman Catholic Church. It was soon after the most recent event that I had a conversation with a friend of mine who was the number one ranking pilot, in terms of seniority, in a major American airline. We were having lunch, and he said, "You're never going to believe what happened to me."

I asked, "What happened?"

He responded, "On my latest trip to Rome, it was the Year of Jubilee. I walked through the door and I met the pope." He started to weep and said, "I received a plenary indulgence so that all the sins I have ever committed were forgiven by the church, by the sacraments, by the power of the keys of St. Peter."

It was clear, as I spoke to this man, that the doctrine of indulgences is still very much a part of the Roman system. It is reaffirmed along with the treasury of merit, purgatory, and like matters in the Catholic catechism.

A few years ago I was in Rome taking a group of people on a tour. The tour guide asked me what I wanted to see most. I told him, "The thing I want to see more than anything else is the Lateran Church."

The tour guide said, "The Lateran Church? What's so special about the Lateran Church?"

I responded, "That is where the Scala Sancta are."

He did not know what that was, so I further explained that these were the sacred steps that the Crusaders brought back from Jerusalem. Supposedly these were the steps that Jesus actually walked on as He went to the judgment hall. They have become an important relic for the Roman Catholic Church. It is believed that if one goes up the stairs on their knees, saying specific prayers on each step, they can receive a significant indulgence.

It was in that exact location, when Luther visited in Rome in 1510, that he had his awakening experience of disillusionment. After he ascended the sacred stairs on his knees, reached the top, and stood up, he said out loud, "Who knows if it is true?" It was at this moment that the seed of Luther's awakening to the gospel of justification by faith alone was planted. I wanted to go and stand where Luther stood and had that crisis moment.

We went to the Lateran Church, but I was unable to get anywhere near the stairs because every square inch of every step was completely covered with pilgrims, most of them elderly, who were on their knees, praying, kissing the steps, and going through the ritual that would give them indulgences and reduce their time in purgatory. There was a plaque beside the stairs that announced the indulgence value of making this pilgrimage. In that moment I thought, *I'd like every American evangelical to see this, because we keep being told that Rome has changed and does not believe in this system anymore.*

A Marred View of Justification

We learn about Catholicism's view of justification by analyzing the sixth session of the Council of Trent, which was dedicated to establishing the canons and decrees concerning justification in the church. The church first defined their view of justification, and then proceeded to list the anathemas, which are the statements of denial following the formula, "If anyone says…," "let him be anathema," meaning, "let him be damned."

When those canons are read carefully, it becomes evident that any orthodox evangelical would be anathematized by the sixth session of the Council of Trent. In their positive exposition of justification we learn of how Rome understands the doctrine. We see that justification begins with the sacrament of baptism. Justification, according to Rome, is imparted sacerdotally, through the ministry of the church via the sacraments—most notably the sacrament of baptism, and secondarily the sacrament of penance.

As Rome spells it out, justification begins with baptism. This may seem a bit technical, but Rome defines baptism as "the instrumental cause of justification." That phrase, "instrumental cause," has its roots in Aristotelian philosophy, which was synthesized in the Middle Ages with Roman Catholic theology. When Aristotle defined motion and causality, he designated several different types of causes: efficient cause, formal cause, instrumental cause, final cause, and so on. He used the illustration of a sculpture.

If a statue is to be beautiful it has to have a material cause; it must be built out of a block of stone, block of wood, or some other material. The efficient cause would be the sculptor who shapes it. The important piece of this puzzle is the instrumental cause; according to Aristotle, it was the instrument or instruments by which the change from a square block of marble into a magnificent statue was brought to pass. The sculptor did not just look at the block of wood and say, "Let there be a statue." Instead, Michelangelo and others had to use tools.

Rome used this language in articulating her theology and wrote, "The instrumental cause of justification is baptism." In the sacrament of baptism, this is what is said to happen: The receiver of the baptism has the grace of justification, or what is sometimes called the righteousness of Christ, infused into the soul, which means it is poured into the soul of the believer. There it resides and inhabits the soul. However, that grace supposedly can be augmented or diminished. Rome has a tendency to speak of that grace in quantitative terms rather than qualitative terms.

In any case, here at the beginning of justification, there is an affirmation that grace and the righteousness of Christ are required, but how the sinner gets that righteousness is through an infusion of grace into the soul. Once that grace is infused, virtually automatically by the sacrament of baptism, then the recipients of baptism must give their cooperation to such an extent that they become actually righteous. Only when righteousness is "inherent" in those individuals (as a result of their cooperation with this infused grace) do they enter a state of justification. God will declare them just or righteous only when righteousness inheres within them.

Please note that they could not be righteous without the infusion of the righteousness of Christ, but they also could not be righteous without their own cooperation. Once both of these occur, they are righteous and in a state of justification, in which they remain unless or until they commit mortal sin.

Center of Controversy

The Roman Catholic Church distinguishes between mortal and venial sin. Venial sin is real sin, but it is not serious enough to kill the justifying grace that is in the soul. Mortal sin is called mortal because it kills or destroys the grace of justification. Some of the mortal sins in Roman Catholic theology are adultery, murder, stealing, drunkenness, and missing mass on Sunday. If an individual commits one of these sins, then he loses his justification.

One would then think that if a person lost his justification through mortal sin that the remedy would be to go back to the church and say, "Baptize me again." But Rome believes that even though someone may lose his justification, he still maintains an indelible mark from his original baptism. The sinner is not baptized again, but instead, the remedy comes from what the church defines as the second plank of justification, the sacrament of penance, "for those who have made shipwreck of their souls." It was the sacrament of penance that was at the center of the controversy in the sixteenth century that brought about the biggest schism in the history of Christendom.

To be clear, the sacrament of penance has several components to it, including confession, absolution, and works of satisfaction.

When I talk with evangelicals and ask, "What is the difference between you and a Catholic?" the most common response is this: "I don't have to go to confession." Yet that is not the most prominent difference, for Christians should not be opposed to confessing sins. The New Testament advises us to confess our sins one to another. Even Luther kept the confessional in the sixteenth century. We are uncomfortable with a priest saying, "I absolve you" because we acknowledge that we have but one priest, and it is Jesus Christ alone who gives anyone absolution.

But as evangelicals, once again we have to be careful to not paint a caricature, for historically, the Roman Catholic Church does not believe that the priest has some kind of inherent magical power to forgive sins. Priestly absolution, in terms of their doctrine, is what is understood as the priest speaking on behalf of Christ by announcing Christ's forgiveness of sins to those who repent.

At the time of the Reformation, it was not absolution and it was not confession that created the firestorm. It was the next part of penance, the works of satisfaction, which are necessary for the sacrament to work. As an integral and necessary part of the sacrament, the repentant sinner, to be restored to the state of justification, is required to perform certain works to satisfy the demands of God. When these works are completed, the sinner receives a specific type of merit that is needed to restore his standing before God.

It is helpful to note that there are different categories or types of merit. *Condign merit* is merit of such a high level of virtue that it imposes an obligation upon God, who is just and righteous to reward it. *Congruous merit* is merit good enough that it would be congruous or "fitting" for God to restore justification to an individual. *Supererogatory merit* is above and beyond what God requires of His people. There have been just a handful of people in history who, according to Rome, when they died, were in such a state of righteousness that they went directly to heaven.

The Antithesis of Biblical Justification

The overwhelming majority of people who die, even though they do not die in a state of mortal sin, still have abiding impurities on their soul. And as long as an individual has impurities in his life at the time of death, instead of going to heaven, he goes to purgatory, which is called purgatory because it is the place of purging—where impurities are cleansed. It is in purgatory that the impure man is molded, shaped, and made righteous enough to get into heaven. Some individuals may spend only a few hours in purgatory, while others may be there for years, and some even up to millions of years.

If I had to go to purgatory to be cleansed of the impurities that remain in my life, I would have a hard time knowing when my parole date was due. This reminds me of a time when I was introduced by John MacArthur at a conference. John said,

> Before I give my address, I have to confess this dreadful dream that I had last night. I dreamed that I died and I stood before the gates of heaven. There was Peter, and he said, "John, we have been waiting for you. We expected you, but we have a little exercise you have to go through before you can get in."
>
> Peter pointed over to the side, and there was a large ladder that stretched up through the clouds as far as the eye could see. He said, "You have to go over there and climb that ladder, and you

have to put a mark on every rung for every sin that you have committed in your life." Angels came over to me carrying a big white log of chalk. And they put this log on my shoulder, and I could barely lift it, but I balanced it there.

I got on the ladder and I leaned forward and checked the first rung. Then I went up and checked the second rung. I was on that ladder for two weeks and I could see no diminution in the size of that log. All of a sudden, I saw movement above me. I had to move my hand, because there was a foot coming down the ladder. I looked up...and it was R.C. Sproul coming down for more chalk.

We all had a good laugh. But beloved, there is not enough chalk in the world to get me to the top of that ladder. That is why the Roman Catholic gospel is no gospel. It is horrible news, and I would despair altogether in that schema. Luther said the true gospel has no place for the sinner claiming merit of any kind before almighty God; the only merit that can save is the merit of Christ and Christ alone.

Yet many poor souls have sought to gain merit in purgatory through indulgences. People in the Middle Ages made arduous journeys to Rome and to other places in order to receive indulgences that would supposedly reduce their sentence or their loved one's sentence in purgatory. It is no wonder these people were driven to visit every place that had relics.

Frederick III, the Elector of Saxony, wanted his university in Wittenberg to rival all the other universities in Germany and in Europe. He had the same goal for his relic collection in Wittenberg. He had amassed more than 15,000 relics, and spent a fortune to bring them to Wittenberg. His collection included what was said to be a vial of milk from the breast of the Virgin Mary, pieces of the cross, and a hair from the beard of John the Baptist. The indulgence value of the collection of relics in Wittenberg at the time of the Reformation was said to be 1,907,000 years. Which meant that if a pilgrim came to Wittenberg and looked at each relic there, he could buy 1,907,000 years of time off from purgatory. The alarming thing about this is that the largest professing body of Christendom still practices it.

These indulgences could take time off of a purgatory sentence only by getting merit from the treasury of merit, which is like a celestial bank account in which the excess merits of a few are deposited. I mentioned earlier that the average person is going to spend a long time in purgatory before he gets to heaven, but Rome claims there are a few people who live lives that are righteous enough that they go directly to heaven. In fact, there are some in church history who are said to have been so righteous that they have accrued for themselves a surplus of merit—people like St. Francis, St. Augustine, Francis Xavier, and Thomas Aquinas. Their surplus is deposited into the treasury of merit, and it is the church in general, and the pope in particular, who has the keys of the kingdom and access to that treasury of merit. Therefore, the pope has the authority to make withdrawals and apply those merits to people who are deficient in their righteousness.

Much of this system stems from when the church was building St. Peter's Basilica in Rome and it needed the finances to do so. One of the works of satisfaction tied to the sacrament of penance was the giving of alms. If a person was truly sorry for his sins and wanted to be restored to justification, one of the things he could do was show the sincerity of his repentance by giving alms to the church.

A Monk and a Mallet

In the sixteenth century, Rome had made it clear that these indulgences were not to be understood as salvation for sale. The peasants were supposed to have it explained to them that the only way they would get these indulgences was if their alms-giving was from a true spirit of penitence, and not out of a crass sense of trying to buy their way into heaven.

Justification is by faith alone, not by faith and something else. Justification is by grace alone. Justification is by Christ alone.

However, the representative in Germany, Johann Tetzel, did not have time for such subtleties. Instead, he made up his little jingle: "Every time a coin in the kettle rings, a soul from purgatory springs." Luther was outraged and penned the 95 Theses, which mentioned the corruption of the sacrament of penance, the corruption of indulgences, the corruption of the treasury of merit, and raised questions about the whole system of purgatory and even beyond that, the whole system of justification. Luther understood that it was not faith plus works, not grace plus merit, not inherent righteousness plus the righteousness of Christ that becomes the means and the grounds upon which an individual is justified. Luther made use of a single word that became the buzzword of the Reformation—*sola*. Justification is by faith alone, not by faith and something else. Justification is by grace alone. Justification is by Christ alone. And the Reformation was off and running.

Catholic Faith and Justification

The Roman Catholic Church does not delete faith's role in justification; it just creates an unbiblical perspective of it. The Council of Trent stressed the necessity of faith in order to be justified. According to Trent, faith helps justification in three ways: Faith is the *initium*, the *fundamentum*, and the *radix* of justification.

Faith being the *initium* of justification means that it initiates but does not accomplish justification. That is to say, it is a necessary condition for justification, but it is not a sufficient condition for justification. You cannot be justified without it, but its mere presence is not enough to justify you. Sadly, in Rome's view, a person can have true faith and not possess justification.

Second, faith is the *fundamentum*—that is, the foundation upon which justification is established. We would disagree and state that when true faith is present, it has the certificate of occupancy already because all that is necessary for justification has taken place because our faith is in Christ, who justifies the sinner.

Third, faith is the *radix* or the root of justification. Apparently you can have the initiation of justification, the foundation of justification, and the root of justification, yet no true justification. The only time and only way God will ever declare anyone just is if and when that person actually is just, according to Rome.

How lacking is this system of belief. A person gets a quick dose of justification at baptism. It lasts as long as the individual refrains from committing mortal sin. If mortal sin is committed, that person loses his justification, but can retrieve it through the sacrament of penance. If the individual has enough righteousness that inheres in his soul, he can go to heaven. If there is mortal sin left when he dies, he goes to hell. But if he is merely impure, he goes to purgatory. Not until after the purging flames of that place cleanse him of his impurities is he finally worthy to enter into the kingdom of God.

Clinging to the True Gospel

The Roman Catholic gospel is no gospel. For there is no other gospel except the gospel that is set forth clearly for us in the New Testament. The day the Roman Church anathematized justification by faith alone, it anathematized itself. When the church in the Middle Ages committed apostasy, it stopped being the church.

Many ecumenical movements are arising. Even professing evangelicals are saying, as they join hands with members of the Roman Catholic Church, that they have a unity of faith in the gospel. I have said to them, "If you have a unity of faith in the gospel with these people, you do not have a unity of faith in the gospel with me." Why? Because the Roman Catholic Church is embracing the Tridentine Doctrine of Trent, their view of the gospel, which ultimately denies the gospel of Jesus Christ.

Beloved, if you are unwilling to contend for this, then get out of the way because you are pleasing men rather than Christ. Luther warned that this would happen, just as Jude, Peter, and Paul warned us too. Luther said at the end of his life that his great fear was that the light that had burst forth with the rediscovery of the gospel would go out again in the next generation, that the gospel would be eclipsed into obscurity. Why is there a temptation to let this happen? Because anytime the gospel is preached boldly and accurately, it creates conflict, and as human beings, we naturally want to avoid conflict with others.

But the reality is that doctrine divides. It divided the prophets of Israel from the false prophets. It divided Jesus from the Pharisees. It divided the apostles from those who despised them. Anyone who has ever stayed the course of the gospel has known and will know conflict. At some point, we have to say with Luther, who in "A Mighty Fortress Is Our God" penned the words, "Let goods and kindred go, this mortal life also." Forsaking all, we cling to the gospel of Jesus Christ, for there is no hope elsewhere.

I did not grow up in an evangelical Christian home. I grew up in the heart of paganism. Christ saved me while I was still a sinner. He looked and found no inherent righteousness in me.

I understood right away that my only hope in life was in Christ. If I had to wait to become righteous or to be counted righteous, my condition was utterly hopeless. You take away justification by faith alone from me, you are taking away Christ and His gospel.

My dear friends, you must not shrink from this battle. God will hold you accountable on the last day. Proclaim the whole counsel of God to every one of those people whom God has entrusted to your care. You cannot love the world so much that you allow the gospel to go into eclipse. For that is no love at all. Remember Paul's warning: "Even if we, or an angel from heaven, should preach to you a gospel contrary to what we have preached to you, he is to be accursed" (Galatians 1:8).

Our Monument

If you go to Geneva today you can visit the Reformation Wall, a huge wall that commemorates the Reformation. Chiseled into the wall are the words *Post Tenebras Lux*, Latin for "After darkness, light." My great fear is that the monument of our age will read, "After the light, darkness." May it never be. Master the gospel of justification by faith alone in Christ alone. And make sure that your people understand it in its fullness.

PRAYER

Father, we understand that we stand before You by grace alone, through faith alone, and in Christ alone. We pray that You would increase our love for the sweetness of that gospel, that we might have a clearer understanding of it and a passion to communicate and defend it wherever that battle rages. We ask You in Jesus' name and for His sake. Amen.

THE EXTENT OF THE ATONEMENT

"[He] is the Savior of all men, especially of believers."
1 TIMOTHY 4:10

7

THE EXTENT OF THE ATONEMENT

Phil Johnson
Shepherds' Conference 2003

Selected Scriptures

For whom did Christ die? Did the Good Shepherd give His life for the sheep, or did He die for all people without exception? Did He merely make forgiveness possible for anyone and everyone, or did He actually secure redemption for the elect? What, precisely, did God intend to accomplish through the death of His Son—and will His design be fully realized? Above all, is there a limit to the worth or value of the atoning sacrifice Christ offered?

Those questions are all part of the perennial debate between Calvinists and Arminians regarding the extent of the atonement. They are important and valid questions—but only if we can first agree on the question of *how* the death of Christ made atonement for sin.

Scripture says "Christ died for our sins" (1 Corinthians 15:3)—"the just for the unjust" (1 Peter 3:18). God "made Him who knew no sin to be sin on our behalf, so that we might become the righteousness of God in Him" (2 Corinthians 5:21). "Christ redeemed us from the curse of the Law, having become a curse for us" (Galatians 3:13). He "was delivered over because of our transgressions" (Romans 4:25). "He was pierced through for our transgressions, He was crushed for our iniquities; the chastening for our well-being fell upon Him" (Isaiah 53:5).

Those statements are clear, and this is by far the most vital truth to understand about the crucifixion: *It was a substitutionary sacrifice.* Christ died in the place and in the stead of those whom He saves. His death on the cross paid the penalty of their sin in full. He suffered everything condemned sinners deserve under the wrath of almighty God. In return He gives believers a right standing before God, with immense, eternal blessings that only He rightfully deserves. Those who trust Him alone as Savior are spiritually united with Him, and His righteousness counts as theirs. Having fully atoned for their sins, He now covers them with the glorious garment of His own absolute perfection.

One's view of the *extent* of the atonement is comparatively insignificant next to the all-important truth that Christ's suffering and death were a vicarious payment of sin's penalty—a *penal substitution.* On that issue all truly evangelical Protestants have historically been in full agreement. Individuals and denominations who have experimented with alternative theories about the atonement have invariably drifted into liberalism, pietism, sacerdotalism, or other forms of works-based religion. In other words, when someone abandons the principle of penal substitution, that person has already moved outside the circle of evangelical orthodoxy.

On the other hand, if you accept the fact that Christ's death on the cross was a penal substitution, you have already affirmed the central principle underlying the historic Calvinist position on the extent of the atonement. The Calvinist view is often referred to as "limited atonement," but that's an unfortunate and misleading name. It's an expression invented for the sake of the TULIP acronym (a mnemonic device for remembering the so-called "five points of Calvinism"). But to describe the atonement as "limited" wrongly gives the impression that Calvinists believe the sacrifice Christ offered was of finite value. That is emphatically not the case.

The Five Points

To speak of "the five points of Calvinism" is likewise misleading. John Calvin never outlined the doctrines of grace in five points, nor was he personally involved in the debate from which the five points arose. The Arminians—followers of James Arminius—were responsible for singling out and highlighting the five points. Nearly a half-century after Calvin's death they brought a complaint against the teaching of the Reformed churches of Holland. Their protest was delivered in the form of a document known as the Five Articles of Remonstrance. In response, the Reformed church convened the Synod of Dort in 1618, and they issued a list of written replies organized under the five heads of doctrine suggested by the Arminian remonstrants' five objections. The Canons of the Synod of Dort is therefore the original and definitive source of the principles popularly known as the five points of Calvinism.

It's not clear who first arranged the five points under the acronym TULIP. The arrangement seems to date back to the early twentieth century. It's an easy way to remember the five points but perhaps not the best way to understand them accurately.

The *T* stands for *total depravity.* That's the common theological shorthand label used to signify this principle, but it can be somewhat misleading. To say the human race is fallen and "totally depraved" is not to suggest that all people are as bad as they could possibly be. The idea instead is that sin has infected every aspect of our being: mind, emotions, will, body, soul, imagination, subconscious—and every other faculty capable of giving vent to what's in our hearts. Some prefer to use the expression "total inability," stressing the fact that sinners are so infected with sin that they cannot please God (Romans 8:8). That's what we mean when we say human depravity is total. It is an utter inability to do anything good to earn favor with God. Sin poisons the whole person. What we do, what we think, what we love, what we choose—all of it is contaminated with sin. We are thoroughly sinful. That doesn't mean we are as evil as we could possibly be. It just means that no part of our being is free from the taint of sin.

U is for *unconditional election.* This means God chooses who will be saved, and He does it not because of anything good He finds in the sinner. Lots of people try to tiptoe around the doctrine of election, but you can't do that and be faithful to the biblical text. Ephesians 1:4 distinctly says that God "chose us in Him before the foundation of the world." Furthermore, election is unconditional in the sense that it is not based on some foreseen act of faith (or any other good thing in the person whom God chooses). It is determined solely by the good pleasure of God's own choice. According to Ephesians 1:11, we are "predestined according to His purpose who works all things after the counsel of His will." We don't elect ourselves by responding to the gospel. God chose us before time began. We were sovereignly drawn to Christ, as Jesus told the disciples in John 15:16: "You did not choose Me but I chose you." The expression *unconditional election* stresses the fact that God's choice was determinative. "We love, because He first loved us" (1 John 4:19).

L stands for *limited atonement.* This, of course, is the doctrine we are chiefly concerned with, and as noted, I'm not fond of the expression. *Particular redemption* is a more suitable term, stressing the fact that God had a definite plan in the atonement, and His design will be fully accomplished. (It's worth noting that *everyone,* even the rankest Arminian, believes the atonement is limited in some sense—unless you want to opt for a universal atonement, where everyone without exception will ultimately be saved. The notion of a completely *un*limited atonement is patently unbiblical.)

The *I* stands for *irresistible grace,* and this is another expression that sometimes misleads people. Dave Hunt claimed that those who call grace irresistible are in effect suggesting that God employs force or violence against the free will of whoever He draws to Christ. But that idea is expressly repudiated in virtually every classic Calvinist doctrinal statement. The Westminster Confession of Faith, for example, emphatically says that while God is absolutely sovereign, "neither is God the author of sin, nor is violence offered to the will of the creatures" (WCF 3.1). Rather, grace is "irresistible" in the same way we might say the laughter of a happy infant is irresistible. God's grace draws people by attraction; He does not compel us by force. He opens our eyes to the glory of Christ, and we find that glory *irresistible.* The actual point is that God's saving grace is always *effectual.* Jesus said in John 6:37, "All that the Father gives Me will come to Me." God will not fail to save those whom He elects.

And finally, the *P* in TULIP is for *perseverance of the saints.* The biblical doctrine of perseverance teaches that those who are in Christ will never fully or finally fall away (1 John 2:19). This doctrine seems particularly confusing for some. By no means should we ever imagine that we as believers might summon the power to persevere in the faith by our own power or through the independent exercise of human free will. Nor does it mean that a person can abandon the faith and yet remain certain of salvation and eternal security. Those who do fall away give irrefutable proof that they never really knew Christ (1 John 2:19). True believers always persevere, because God graciously *keeps* us in the faith. We "are protected by the power of God through faith for a salvation ready to be revealed in the last time" (1 Peter 1:5). It's not that the saints have any ability to hold fast by their own power, but that God's grace sovereignly secures their perseverance. He is the one "who is able to keep you from stumbling, and to make you stand in the presence of His glory blameless with great joy" (Jude 24).

Those are the doctrines popularly known as the five points of Calvinism. I affirm them all, insofar as they are properly understood in light of Scripture.

But recognizing that many stumble when they encounter the principle commonly referred to as limited atonement, we need to take a closer look at that doctrine and consider carefully what the Bible says about it.

Particular Redemption

First, let's acknowledge that this issue is the most difficult of all the five points to understand and accept. At least four out of five Calvinists will say that this is the last of the five points they came to grips with. It is not an easy issue, and we should not pretend that it is.

Second, because this is not a simple issue, it should not be considered simplistically. It's vital to understand that there is not just one view for the limited atonement position and another view for the unlimited atonement position, as if there are two polar opposites that compete against each other. This is not really an "either-or" question, even among Calvinists. In fact, historically, the most intense debates about limited atonement have been intramural, among people who hold to different flavors of Calvinism. There are at least three major divisions of Calvinists: high, moderate, and low Calvinists. They all have different views, and there are many shades and degrees in between. In fact, I doubt if you could find any two Calvinists who agree completely with one another on every text and every nuance related to this topic.

Questions related to the extent of the atonement caused a huge debate among Calvinists during the Marrow Controversy in Scotland in the 1700s. This was also one of the major issues on which Andrew Fuller

contended with other Calvinistic Baptists during the late eighteenth century in England. It has been continual fodder for debate among Welsh
Calvinists since the beginning of the 1700s. In 2002, The Banner of Truth
Trust published the first English version of a classic Welsh book on this
issue, *The Atonement Controversy in Welsh Theological Literature and Debate,*
1707–1841.

If you want to sample some moderate opinions on the extent of the
atonement from leading mainstream Calvinist writers, read what Andrew
Fuller, Thomas Boston, Robert L. Dabney, William G.T. Shedd, B.B.
Warfield, and Charles Hodge wrote on the subject. They may surprise you.
Read John Owen too, but do not imagine that Owen's book *The Death of*
Death in the Death of Christ represents the only strain of Calvinist thought
on the issue. It does not—in fact, far from it.

Anyone who studies this issue in depth will quickly discover that the
classic Calvinist view on the extent of the atonement is a lot less narrow
and a lot less cut-and-dried than some of today's young, aggressive Calvinists would like to admit. Historic Calvinism as a movement has generally
acknowledged that there *are* universal aspects of the atonement. Calvin
himself clearly did not hold the rigid views some of today's ultra-high Calvinists are trying to defend on the Internet. Despite what you might read
in some of those militant Internet discussions, it's not necessarily unorth-
odox or anti-Calvinistic to "testify that the Father has sent the Son to be
the Savior of the world" (1 John 4:14).

Let me also admit that this is one issue where historical theology is not
overwhelmingly on the side of the Calvinists. Until some of the later Catholic scholastics raised this question and began to debate about it in the
Middle Ages, most of the church fathers and leading theological writers
in the church, both orthodox and heretical, assumed that Christ died for
all humanity and that was the end of that. There are some exceptions, like
Theodoret of Cyrus (AD 393–466), who wrote this about Hebrews 9:27-
28: "It should be noted, of course, that [Christ] bore the sins of many, not
of all: not all came to faith so He removed the sins of the believers only."[1]

Ambrose (AD 339–397), wrote, "Although Christ suffered for all,
yet He suffered for us particularly, because He suffered for the church."[2]
Jerome (AD 347–420), a contemporary of Augustine, commented on

Matthew 20:28: "He does not say that he gave his life for all, but for many, that is, for all those who would believe."[3] Those are classic Calvinist statements. You can find little remarks like that here and there among the church fathers, but for the most part, when they wrote about the atonement, they treated it as universal.

My friend Curt Daniel has written an excellent syllabus that I want to recommend, titled *The History and Theology of Calvinism* (Dallas: Scholarly Reprints, 1993). It is the best single overview of Calvinism I have encountered. It is filled with copious quotations and wonderful insight, and he covers the differing opinions Calvinists have expressed regarding how to explain the universal and particular aspects of the atonement. Another resource I recommend is Paul Helm's *Calvin & the Calvinists* (Edinburgh: Banner of Truth, 1982). This work makes a persuasive case to show that Calvin himself was indeed a five-point Calvinist. Several popular authors have tried to argue otherwise, but Helm convincingly refutes their thesis.

I'll cite just one quotation that settles the question of whether Calvin held to the doctrine of particular redemption. Commenting on 1 John 2:2, he wrote, "Under the word *all* or whole, he does not include the reprobate, but designates those who should believe as well as those who were then scattered through various parts of the world."[4]

I have said all this to stress that this is the most despised and controversial of all the teachings of Calvinism. And even among Calvinists, there is a lot of debate.

Infinitely Sufficient

Now, you may be asking, "If you admit that this wasn't held by many of the church fathers and only loosely held by Calvin himself, why make an issue out of it at all?" Because there is an important point of truth in seeing how the atoning work of Christ applies to the elect in a particular sense by the design and purpose of God.

The average person thinks this debate is all about the sufficiency and the value of Christ's atoning work, but that is not the disagreement. In the Second Head, Article 3 of Canons of the Synod of Dort we read, "The death of the Son of God is the only and most perfect sacrifice and satisfaction for sin, and is of infinite worth and value, abundantly sufficient to expiate the sins of the whole world." That is the canonical Calvinist manifesto. Calvinists have *always* believed and emphatically affirmed that the sacrifice of Christ was of infinitely sufficient value.

In other words, if one more person had been elect, Christ would not have had to suffer more than He did. Not one more blow from the Roman scourge would have been necessary. Not one more thorn would have been added to His crown. He would not have needed to spend one more moment under God's wrath in order to atone for those additional souls, even if God *had* sovereignly chosen to save every person who ever lived. Not only that, but if God had intended to redeem Adam alone and leave the rest of us to bear the curse and the punishment of our sin in eternal hell, Christ would have not had to suffer any less than He did. Infinite value, by definition, cannot be diminished or added to in any respect.

I occasionally meet Calvinists who bristle or balk whenever someone says the atonement Christ offered was "sufficient for the whole world but efficacious only for the elect." But to say that is simply to affirm an important truth that the Canons of the Synod of Dort specifically singled out and stressed—namely, that the death of Christ was of infinite value and dignity.

Now, I should mention that there are indeed a few Calvinists who hold to a limited-sufficiency view of the atonement. They do not like saying that the atonement is of infinite value. Tom Nettles, for example, does not seem to agree with the Synod of Dort on this. In the book *By His Grace and for His Glory*, Nettles traces the roots of Calvinist doctrine throughout Baptist history. I recommend the book even though I would disagree strongly with Nettles on this point about the atonement. Nettles argues that if Christ's death was substitutionary, then He died for particular sins of particular people. If He died for particular sins, then He did not die for other sins than those. Nettles seems to see such a one-for-one equivalence between our sins and the price of their atonement that he denies the sufficiency of the atonement to save anyone but those for whom it was designed to save. He writes, "The just nature of God does not permit him to inflict more wrath on the substitute than actually becomes effectual for forgiveness of the criminal. Nor does the love of God for the Son permit such an overkill."[5] Nettles apparently holds a view that some would call *equivalentism*. It is the notion that Christ suffered just so much, a finite amount in relation to the sins of the elect.

It pains me to disagree with Tom Nettles, but it needs to be said that his position stands in opposition to the Synod of Dort and the mainstream of historic Calvinism. His basic argument is that if Christ's atonement was substitutionary, then it had to be for particular sins and therefore it had a specific, finite value. I would argue instead that if the atonement Christ offered is substitutionary, then it *had to be of infinite value* for two reasons. One, as the Synod of Dort points out, the Person who submitted to the punishment on our behalf was not only really a man and perfectly holy, but also the only begotten Son of God, of the same eternal and infinite essence with the Father and the Holy Spirit. Because the Person who died on the cross was infinite in His glory and His goodness, His death was an infinite sacrifice.

Second, the punishment due each person for sin is endless wrath. An eternity in hell is not sufficient to atone for sin. So the price of atonement is infinite, and therefore the atonement itself, in order to be accepted, had to be of infinite value. That is precisely what the principle of *penal substitution* means—that Christ bore an immeasurable outpouring of divine wrath on the cross, taking on Himself everything sinners deserve. If Christ's death was not sufficient to atone for all, then it was not sufficient to atone for even one—because atonement for sin, even for one person, demands an infinite price.

The Crux of the Matter

The real debate between Calvinists and Arminians is not about the *sufficiency* of the atonement. The real issue is the design and the application of the atonement. Was it God's purpose to save specific people, or was He trying indiscriminately to save as many people as possible? What was His intent? What was His design? *Did Christ's death perfectly fulfill the plan of redemption as God ordained it?*

If you answer that question yes, you are affirming the principle underlying the Calvinistic position. Here are some even more important questions: Will all of God's purposes for sending Christ to die ultimately be accomplished? Did God intend something by the atonement that will not come to pass? Is there any divinely ordained purpose in Christ's dying that will ultimately be frustrated? Asking those questions puts the importance of the whole issue in a totally different and clearer light.

The earliest Christians firmly believed, as I do, that the death of Christ will accomplish everything God's hand and His purpose predestined (Acts 4:28)—no more, no less. If we believe God is truly sovereign, we must ultimately come to that position. God is not going to be frustrated throughout all eternity because He was desperately trying to save some people who just could not be persuaded. That is how many Christians think redemption works. It is a grossly unbiblical way of thinking about God. The one true God who reveals Himself in Scripture says He planned and ordained the end of all things before the beginning of time, and He distinctly adds this: "My purpose will be established, and I will accomplish all My good pleasure" (Isaiah 46:10).

Christ's atoning work also accomplishes no *more* than God intended it to accomplish. If benefits accrue to nonbelievers because of Christ's death, then it is because God designed it that way. If Christ's dying means that the judgment of the whole world is postponed, then unregenerate people reap the benefits and the blessings of common grace *through the atonement.* That is exactly the outcome God designed. It did not happen by accident.

So this is my position (and it has been the teaching of most Calvinists throughout history): Some benefits of the atonement are universal, and some benefits of the atonement are particular and limited to the elect alone.

Substitutionary Atonement

It is important to mention that ultimately, we cannot escape the limited and particular aspects of the atonement if we believe Christ's death on the cross was substitutionary. Let me illustrate: Did Christ suffer for Pharaoh's sins in Pharaoh's place and in his stead? Certainly not, because when Christ died on the cross, Pharaoh was already in hell suffering for his own sin. Those who suffer in hell all suffer for their own sin. Christ does not suffer on their behalf in the same way He did for people who are ultimately redeemed and delivered from hell. That's a rather obvious point, if you think about it.

The substitutionary aspects of the atonement therefore ultimately belong to the elect alone. Jesus bore their punishments so that they will not have to. If He had suffered vicariously for the sins of Judas in the same way He suffered in Peter's place, then Judas would not be suffering right now for his own sins. That is the inevitable ramification of vicarious atonement.

Universal Ramifications

At the same time, there are universal aspects of the atoning work of Christ, and historic Calvinism has always recognized this. That is exactly the meaning of 1 Timothy 4:10, which is perhaps the best, clearest text in all of Scripture to settle this whole question: "We have fixed our hope on the living God, who is the Savior of all men, especially of believers." R.B. Kuiper famously said he preferred to speak of Christ's dying *especially* for the elect rather than *only* for them. He wrote, "God designed to save *the elect* through the death of His Son...[But] the statement, so often heard from Reformed pulpits, that Christ died *only* for the elect must be rated a careless one."[6] To those who believe, Christ is Savior in a special and particular sense. His death had a particular reference to them in the ultimate design of God.

Curt Daniel gives a helpful illustration of how this is true by pointing to the parable in Matthew 13:44: "The kingdom of heaven is like a treasure hidden in the field, which a man found and hid again; and from joy over it he goes and sells all that he has and buys that field." Buying the field ensures that the man buys the treasure. The treasure was the object and the aim of his purchase. The treasure was the reason for His great joy. The treasure was the reason He made this deal in the first place. But He did not purchase the treasure only; He purchased the whole field. That is a good way, I think, to look at the atoning work of Christ.

Read Romans 14:9: "To this end Christ died and lived again, that He might be Lord both of the dead and of the living." Notice that the verse is teaching us that because of Christ's death and resurrection, He is Lord of all men in a special way. His death on the cross purchased the right for Him, as perfect man and perfect God, to rule as Lord over all the earth— over both the dead and the living, over the redeemed as well as the reprobate. That is also the same message we find in Philippians 2:8-10: "Being found in appearance as a man, He humbled Himself by becoming obedient to the point of death, even death on a cross. For this reason also, God highly exalted Him, and bestowed on Him the name which is above every name, so that at the name of Jesus every knee will bow, of those who are in heaven and on earth and under the earth."

That is a very clear statement that there is a universal ramification of the atonement. Christ's death, in some sense, purchased Him an exalted position of lordship over all. There is a true sense in which Jesus purchased the whole world in order to get the treasure, the church. Meanwhile, there are certain benefits of the atonement that accrue directly to those whom God has not chosen for salvation, the reprobate.

Blessings of Common Grace

Spurgeon said it well in a sermon entitled, "Good Cheer for Many That Fear." He preached, "We believe that by His atoning sacrifice, Christ bought some good things for all men and all good things for some men."[7] What specifically did Spurgeon have in mind when he said that "Christ bought some good things for all men"? Clearly, he was speaking of common grace—the goodness of God and the common blessings of life that are shown to all men. This is the grace that keeps the evil in the world from being as bad as it could possibly be. Common grace is the grace that permits all sinners to live and enjoy life under a temporary reprieve from judgment and justice. Even though sinners are worthy of instant damnation, common grace delays that. Common grace pleads tenderly and earnestly with sinners to repent and to be reconciled to God, even though their hearts are set against Him.

According to Matthew 5:45, "He causes His sun to rise on the evil and the good, and sends rain on the righteous and the unrighteous." God loves the world! For those of you who feel like breaking out the torches and pitchforks whenever someone declares that God loves the whole world, I plead with you to tread lightly, because Scripture does not stop short of stating that truth. This goodness that God shows even to the reprobate is sincere, bona fide, compassionate *love*. It is not the same eternal, redemptive love that God has set on the elect from all eternity. It is love of a different sort, but it is true and genuinely well-meant love nonetheless.

Think carefully about it, and you will realize that every good thing God gives us—including the blessings of common grace—are made possible by the atonement. Because if God had no intention to save anyone ever, He would have instantly damned the whole human race the minute Adam sinned. That is what He did with the angels who fell. They were cast out of heaven at once, and no atonement will ever be made for the sins of any angel.

By contrast, the human race fell, and for the most part, still lives and enjoys life in a world where only we are blessed to an amazing degree with the providential care of a benevolent "God, who richly supplies us with all things to enjoy" (1 Timothy 6:17)—even though we are under the curse of sin. We see beauty and we enjoy the taste of our food. John MacArthur points out that if God wanted to, He could have made all our food taste like sand. But instead, He is good to us. "He Himself gives to all people life and breath and all things" (Acts 17:25). We laugh, experience joy, appreciate love, and we relish the good things of life. All these things are ultimately made possible by the atoning work of Christ. None of them would have been possible at all if Christ had not intended to die to save sinners. God would have instantly damned us all instead. In a superb book on the extent of the atonement, Robert Candlish included a key chapter titled "The Universal Dispensation of Gracious Forbearance—Its Connection with the Atonement," in which he argued persuasively that all the blessings of common grace are made possible by the atoning work of Christ. He wrote,

> It is, then, a great fact, that the death of Christ, or his work of obedience and propitiation, has procured for the world at large, and for every individual—the impenitent and unbelieving as well as the "chosen, and called, and faithful"—certain definite, tangible, and ascertainable benefits; benefits, I mean, not nominal, but real; and not of a vague, but of a well-defined and specific character. Of these the first and chief—that which in truth comprehends all the rest—is the universal grant to all mankind of a season of forbearance, a respite or suspension of judgment, a day or dispensation of grace.[8]

The reprobate therefore benefit from Christ's death, for the crumbs that fall from the table God spreads for His elect are a veritable feast for everyone. They experience all the blessings of common grace. That is a side benefit of the cross and an expression of God's goodness toward sinners.

High Calvinists and hyper-Calvinists sometimes argue that common grace is not really an expression of love or goodness toward the reprobate, because it only increases their damnation. It is true, in the words of Romans 2:4, that unbelievers "think lightly of the riches of His kindness and tolerance and patience"—and they will be held guilty for treating His grace with such contempt. But it is a serious affront to the character of God to suggest that His only purpose in showing common grace to the reprobate is to increase their guilt. One of the most important ways God acts graciously toward the wicked is by restraining the expression of their sinfulness. Most people are not as bad as they could be. None are as bad as they *would* be if God left them to themselves without any grace whatsoever. It should be obvious to anyone who understands human depravity that, on the whole, common grace decreases the severity of human guilt. A.A. Hodge wrote, "The entire history of the human race, from the apostasy to the final judgment, is, as Candlish says, 'a dispensation of forbearance' in respect to the reprobate, in which many blessings, physical and moral, affecting their characters and destinies for ever, accrue even to the heathen."[9]

R.B. Kuiper wrote in a similar vein: "The blessings of common grace, although resulting only indirectly from the atonement, were most surely designed by God to result from the atonement. The design of God in the atoning work of Christ pertained primarily and directly to the redemption of the elect, but indirectly and secondarily it included all the blessings of common grace."[10]

The Free Offer of Salvation

Kuiper identified several universal benefits of the atonement—more than just common grace. For example, he wrote, "No other blessing of the common grace of God is as great as *the universal and sincere offer of salvation*, nor is any other more obviously a fruit of the atonement."[11] He continued, "At no time is the gospel confined to any nation or for that matter, to any particular class of men. It is intended for Jews, Greeks, barbarians, and Scythians."[12]

Scripture supports this truth that the gospel does not discriminate. Colossians 3:11 says, "There is no distinction between Greek and Jew, circumcised and uncircumcised, barbarian, Scythian, slave and freeman." In Matthew 11:28, Jesus said, "Come to Me, all who are weary and heavy-laden, and I will give you rest." About those verses Kuiper wrote, "To say that such invitations…are intended only for those who, having been born again through the grace of the Holy Spirit, have come to realize their lost condition, is to limit the meaning of Scripture without warrant. Let it be said emphatically that the Reformed theology does not teach, as some allege, that the gospel invitation is only for the elect and the regenerate."[13]

There is no necessary contradiction between God's eternal sovereign design to save the elect and His sincere pleas for the reprobate to repent. When we preach the gospel, according to 2 Corinthians 5, it is our duty to plead with all who hear the message that they be reconciled to God. Paul wrote in 2 Corinthians 5:20, "We are ambassadors for Christ, as though God were making an appeal through us; we beg you on behalf of Christ, be reconciled to God." If you are not proclaiming the gospel to everyone with the confidence that they can be saved, you are not a good ambassador for Christ. If you are a Calvinist and you hesitate to extend God's offer of mercy freely to all—if you recoil from inviting men or pleading with them to repent and be reconciled to God—then you are not a good Calvinist.

In Ezekiel 18:23, God says, "Do I have any pleasure in the death of the wicked…rather than that he should turn from his ways and live?" Commenting on that text, Calvin wrote,

> God desires nothing more earnestly than that those who were perishing and rushing to destruction should return into the way of safety. And for this reason not only is the Gospel spread abroad in the world, but God wished to bear witness through all ages how inclined he is to pity…It follows, then, that what the Prophet now says is very true, that God wills not the death of a sinner, because he meets him of his own accord, and is not only prepared to receive all who fly to his pity, but he calls them towards Him with a loud voice, when He sees how they

are alienated from all hope of safety…We hold, then, that God
wills not the death of a sinner, since he calls all equally to repentance, and promises himself prepared to receive them if they
only seriously repent.[14]

Any variety of Calvinism that denies the free offer of salvation is out
of step with John Calvin and a departure from the historic mainstream of
Calvinist conviction. The gospel's call to faith and repentance is meant to
be proclaimed indiscriminately to all. "God is now declaring to men that
all people everywhere should repent" (Acts 17:30).

The Canons of the Synod of Dort expressly affirm that the gospel invitation is to be freely and openly broadcast to all: "The promise of the
gospel is that whosoever believes in Christ crucified shall not perish, but
have eternal life. This promise, together with the command to repent and
believe, ought to be declared and published to all nations, and to all persons promiscuously, and without distinction, to whom God out of His
good pleasure sends the gospel" (Second Head, Article 5).

To sum up, unbelievers receive a number of benefits from the atonement: delayed judgment, all the blessings of common grace, and the free
offer of salvation through the gospel. Those are universal effects of Christ's
atoning work, and that is why Charles Hodge, the great Calvinist theologian, wrote, "There is a sense, therefore, in which [Christ] died for all, and
there is a sense in which He died for the elect alone."[15] That simply echoes
the words of 1 Timothy 4:10: "We have fixed our hope on the living God,
who is the Savior of all men, especially of believers."

Particular Redemption

There is of course a definite, specific reference to the elect in the atoning work of Christ. First Timothy 4:10 plainly states Jesus is "the Savior of
all men," but Jesus is not the Savior of all men equally, for He did not die
for each and every individual alike. "This One is indeed the Savior of the
world" (John 4:42)—but "especially of believers" (1 Timothy 4:10).

Jesus said in John 10:11, "I am the good shepherd; the good shepherd
lays down His life for the sheep." The context makes Jesus' meaning inescapable. The Good Shepherd does not die for the goats or the wolves in

the same way He sacrifices Himself for the sheep. He says it again in verse 15, "I lay down My life *for the sheep.*"

The apostle Paul told the elders at Ephesus, "Be on guard for yourselves and for all the flock, among which the Holy Spirit has made you over-seers, to shepherd the church of God which He purchased with His own blood. I know that after my departure savage wolves will come in among you, not sparing the flock" (Acts 20:28-29). Christ purchased *the church* with His blood. It was those in the church—not the grievous wolves who were threatening the church, but the people of God—who were the object of Christ's affection, and their salvation was the main reason for which He died. The benefits that accrue to the reprobate are secondary effects of that reality.

In what sense did Christ purchase the church? In Ephesians 5:25, Paul used language that evokes the imagery of a marriage price: "Husbands, love your wives, just as Christ also loved the church and gave Himself up for her." For what reason did He purchase her? "So that He might sanc-tify her, having cleansed her by the washing of water with the word, that He might present to Himself the church in all her glory, having no spot or wrinkle or any such thing; but that she would be holy and blameless" (verses 26-27).

Those for whom Christ died are loved with the highest and purest kind of love. It is a particular love, and its closest earthly parallel is the love of a husband for his wife—a type of love that is not dispensed indiscrimi-nately to everyone alike. In fact, what do we call a man who shares conju-gal love with his neighbor and does not reserve it exclusively for his wife? We call him an adulterer. What would you call someone who indiscrimi-nately showed every woman the intense ardent affection men reserve only for their wives? You would call him a philanderer.

Christ's love for His church is pure. It's more tender, more personal, and an infinitely greater love than the love of a husband for his wife.

Here is an excerpt from Curt Daniel's notes on this:

> The key is the analogy of Christ the husband dying for His bride. To understand this, we need to understand the Hebrew concept of marriage. First, the man and the woman were

betrothed to each other. This may have occurred even before either of them were born. Their parents may have arranged the betrothal. From the moment of the betrothal, they were in a sense married…nothing except death or divorce could legally prevent the marriage itself. But before the actual marriage could occur, there had to be an exchange, as it were. The father of the bride provided a dowry, and the groom provided the marriage price. In that sense, the groom "bought" his bride, even though he was already legally obliged to marry her. Then at the appointed time, they came together as man and wife.

This is a perfect type of Christ and the church…The elect were given to Christ by God the Father, and Christ was given to us also by the Father…

But, Christ the groom had to pay the marriage price for His bride. How did he do this? Because of our sins, the price was death. [Christ had to redeem us before He could take us as a bride.] Therefore, Christ gave Himself for the elect in death. The atonement purchased us for Him…

…The order here is crucial. First, Christ loved the church; this is election (vs. 25). Next, he pays the marriage price; this is the atonement (vs. 25). Then, He prepares her for the wedding; this is salvation applied (vs. 26); lastly, He presents her to Himself in marriage; this is the final consummation of our union and glorification (vs. 27).

The point is simply this: Christ died with a special intent for His betrothed that He did not have for the rest of mankind.[16]

Notice that as a part of Jesus' mediatorial work in His high-priestly prayer, Jesus said this: "I do not ask on behalf of the world, but of those whom You have given Me; for they are Yours" (John 17:9). Now remember, when Christ prayed that prayer, He had already entered into the mediatorial office of the high priest. *He expressly excluded the world at large from His high-priestly prayer.* It seems clear from Scripture that Christ's redemptive work had a special reference to His chosen people. When He prayed that prayer, the work of atonement had begun, and He made it a point to exclude the world.

We read in Titus 2:14 that Christ "gave Himself for us to redeem us from every lawless deed, and to purify for Himself a people for His own possession, zealous for good deeds." That statement cannot apply to the reprobate. Did you realize that even your faith is a fruit of the atonement? It is a gift of God (Acts 16:14; Romans 12:3; Philippians 1:29). Even repentance is God's work in us (Acts 5:31; 11:18; 2 Timothy 2:25).

In John 10:26, Jesus said, "You do not believe because you are not of My sheep." Now if Jesus were an Arminian, He would have said, "You are not of My sheep because you believe not." Instead, He said the exact opposite. The Good Shepherd laid down His life for the sheep, and their faith is part of His gift to them.

Jesus said in Matthew 26:28, "This is My blood of the covenant, which is poured out for many for forgiveness of sins." Paul said in Romans 5:15, "The free gift is not like the transgression. For if by the transgression of the one the many died, much more did the grace of God and the gift by the grace of the one Man, Jesus Christ, abound to the many." The author of Hebrews wrote in Hebrews 9:28, "Christ also, having been offered once to bear the sins of many, will appear a second time for salvation without reference to sin, to those who eagerly await Him." Jesus said in John 15:13-14, "Greater love has no one than this, that one lay down his life for his friends. You are My friends if you do what I command you." The reprobate are never called friends of Jesus, but those who do what He commands are His friends; and it is for them that He laid down His life.

Now let me go back to the point I began with: If the atoning work of Christ is substitutionary, it must be limited to those whom Christ actually redeems. In other words, when we understand that the atonement is substitutionary, we must see that in a certain way it applies to particular people. That is the inevitable ramification of vicarious atonement. Again, Christ did not suffer for the sins of Judas in the same way He suffered for Peter's sins. Taking Matthew 26:24 at face value, it seems clear that Judas will suffer for his own sin. "He who does not obey the Son will not see life, but the wrath of God abides on him" (John 3:36). All who die in unbelief will suffer "in their own persons the due penalty of their error" (Romans 1:27). Christ is in no sense their substitute.

Here's another way to say it: The aspects of the atonement that are substitutionary are inherently efficacious. The very reason believers do not have to fear condemnation in the final judgment is that Christ has already paid the price of their sin in full as their substitute. The atonement of Christ did not just make salvation possible; it actually purchased redemption for those who will be saved. He literally bought them, paid their debt, wiped it off the ledger, sealed their pardon, and assured their eternal salvation.

Problem Passages

The key passage referenced by those who reject particular redemption is 1 John 2:2: "He Himself is the propitiation for our sins; and not for ours only, but also for those of the whole world." We have to remember here that the apostle was writing to a primarily Jewish audience. We read in Galatians 2:9, "Recognizing the grace that had been given to me, James and Cephas and John, who were reputed to be pillars, gave to me and Barnabas the right hand of fellowship, so that we might go to the Gentiles and they to the circumcised." That passage reveals that John was an apostle to the Jews. The recipients of his epistles would therefore have been predominantly, if not exclusively, Jewish.

John reminded this Jewish audience that Christ is the propitiation for sins, and not for the sins of Hebrews only, but also for the sins of Gentiles from every tongue and nation throughout the whole world. That's the proper sense of 1 John 2:2. There is little doubt that is exactly how John's initial audience would have understood this expression. The phrase "the whole world" means people of all kinds, including Jews, Gentiles, Greeks, and Romans, as opposed to "ours only," meaning the Jewish nation. The grammatical construction of 1 John 2:2 is an exact parallel to John's analysis of the unwitting prophecy issued by Caiaphas in John 11:51-52: "He prophesied that Jesus was going to die for the nation, and not for the nation only, but in order that He might also gather together into one the children of God who are scattered abroad."

Another verse that those who reject particular redemption turn to is 2 Peter 2:1: " False prophets also arose among the people, just as there will also be false teachers among you, who will secretly introduce destructive heresies, even denying the Master who *bought them*, bringing swift destruction upon themselves." This verse poses no problem if we understand two things.

First, the word "Master" in the phrase "the Master who bought them" is a Greek word that speaks of a sovereign master; it has a strong emphasis on the strength of God's sovereignty and lordship. If you understand this as a reference to Christ, it could simply refer to what Philippians 2:8-10 teaches—that Christ's death obtained for Christ a position of absolute lordship over all. These false teachers who were part of the field Christ purchased in order to obtain the hidden treasure of the church were denying the Lord who bought them. That's one interpretation of the verse.

But nowhere else in the New Testament is this Greek word used to designate Christ. It is an expression normally used to speak of the Father. And if these false teachers were Jewish false teachers, as it appears they were, then Peter may have been paraphrasing an Old Testament passage, Deuteronomy 32:5-6: "They have acted corruptly toward Him, they are not His children, because of their defect; but are a perverse and crooked generation. Do you thus repay the LORD, O foolish and unwise people? *Is not He your Father who has bought you?*" That passage plainly refers to the nation's temporal deliverance from Egypt. Peter may have simply meant that these false teachers were guilty of denying the God who had redeemed their ancestors from the nation of Egypt.

There is a third possible interpretation. Peter may have been making the point simply that although these false teachers had identified with the people of God and claimed to trust Christ, their preaching was a denial of the God they claimed to have been redeemed by.

Those three interpretations are all in perfect harmony with a Calvinistic view of the atonement, and they do not even exhaust the viable interpretations of 2 Peter 2:1. Moreover, the point of the verse is about the enormity of these false teachers' wickedness; it is not about the extent of the atonement. So the verse proves nothing against the Calvinistic doctrine of particular redemption.

An Amazing and Uplifting Truth

Years of wearying debate over limited atonement (much of it unnecessarily acrimonious) has left many Christians with the uneasy feeling that questions about the design and extent of the atonement raise matters best avoided for the sake of peace in the church. It is unfortunate that the doctrine of particular redemption is so controversial, because in reality it is a truth that can only strengthen one's faith that all things do indeed work together for good for those who love God. It underscores the personal nature of God's love for His elect. It greatly clarifies the doctrine of election. It illuminates *all* the doctrines of grace, for that matter.

My appeal to pastors and church leaders with regard to this doctrine is twofold: On the one hand, don't run away *from* this doctrine. It's neither as confusing nor as divisive as you might think. On the other hand, don't run away *with* it. Too many treat this doctrine as if it nullified everything Scripture teaches about common grace and the general benevolence of our loving God. It does not.

Remember, "The LORD is good to all, and His mercies are over all His works" (Psalm 145:9). "He causes His sun to rise on the evil and the good, and sends rain on the righteous and the unrighteous" (Matthew 5:45). But to the elect in particular, Jesus said, "Do not be afraid, little flock, for your Father has chosen gladly to give you the kingdom" (Luke 12:32). "Many are called, but few are chosen" (Matthew 22:14). There is glorious comfort and encouragement in all those truths, for those who have eyes to see.

He "is the Savior of all men, *especially* of believers" (1 Timothy 4:10).

A Biblical Case for Elder Rule

"Be on guard for yourselves and for all the flock,
among which the Holy Spirit has made you overseers,
to shepherd the church of God."

Acts 20:28

A BIBLICAL CASE FOR ELDER RULE

Tom Pennington
Shepherds' Conference 2003

Selected Scriptures

everal years ago I watched a brief film entitled *Unlocking the Mystery of Life*. It described the journey of several scientists away from evolution to intelligent design. The focus of the video, which will never likely be a bestseller, was the bacterial flagellum—a tiny hair that protrudes from a single-cell bacterium. It is what enables the bacteria to move. When it is viewed under powerful electron microscopes, amazingly it is clear that the entire flagellum assembly is a tiny motor! It has all the components of the motors that run our electrical appliances—and the hair serves as a simple rotor.

When I saw the complexity of one single-celled bacterium, I was not only awed that our God has produced such amazing variety in creation, but I was also struck with the reality that He is a God of order—order we witness in even the smallest cells. In fact, the video went on to show that every human cell contains a number of tiny motors, including even a sophisticated DNA assembly line. That is how God designed the human body.

Meticulous Design

Given that our God is a God of meticulous order, even down to the smallest living thing He has made, it surprises me to hear church leaders say that how the church is structured is unimportant. For example, George Barna writes, "The Bible does not rigidly define the corporate practices, rituals, or structures that must be embraced in order to have a proper church."[1] Likewise, Donald Miller writes, "No particular structure of church life is divinely ordained."[2] So God cares about the structure of the bacterial flagellum but doesn't care about how the church—the only entity that He promised to build and bless—is structured?

Miller adds: "Any form which the Holy Spirit can inhabit and to which He may impart the life of Christ must be accepted as valid for the church. As all forms of life adapt themselves to their environment, so does the life of Christ by His Spirit in the church."[3] That is evolutionary theory applied to the structure of the church. Some churches may have a kind of government that is best described as survival of the fittest, but that is not a biblically ordained structure.

Although some dismiss the structure of church government as unimportant, this issue is absolutely crucial, because structure determines how people think and act. As Alexander Strauch writes in *Biblical Eldership*,

> Some of the worst havoc wrought to the Christian faith has been a direct result of unscriptural forms of church structure. Only a few centuries after the apostles' death, for example, Christian churches began to assimilate both Roman and Jewish concepts of status, power, and priesthood…Under Christ's name an elaborately structured institution emerged that corrupted the simple, family structure of the apostolic churches, robbed God's people of their lofty position and ministry in Christ, and exchanged Christ's supremacy over His people for the supremacy of the institutional church.[4]

What should matter most to us is what Scripture says about the structure of the church and its leadership. The church will always have some structure, but what structure—if any—does Scripture prescribe? I want to consider the evidence that in Scripture the normal pattern is a plurality of godly men leading each church. And then I want to examine the biblical evidence that God intends for every church to follow that pattern. But first let's survey the primary models of church government in contemporary Christianity.

Forms of Church Government

Episcopalian

The Episcopalian model maintains that there are three legitimate church offices: bishops, presbyters (also called rectors or priests), and deacons. In this model, bishops alone have the authority to appoint other bishops, presbyters, and deacons. This is a hierarchy in which men outside a local church usually choose those who will lead each church.

Some Episcopalians trace the authority of the bishop back to the apostles, or apostolic succession. Other Episcopalians don't attempt to trace succession back to the apostles but argue it appeared very early in church history and that lends weight to this position. Still others embrace this model because they think it is functionally the best for the structure and organization of the church.

There are four primary denominations that practice this form of church government: the Orthodox, the Anglicans, the Roman Catholics, and some Methodist denominations. The defense for this model is primarily church history. For example, J.B. Lightfoot wrote about the office of bishop, "History seems to show decisively that before the middle of the second century each church or organized Christian community had its three orders of ministers, its bishop, its presbyters, and its deacons."[5] So the Episcopalian form of government likely began in the early 200s, and by the 300s the three offices were common.

Others argue that in Acts 15 James exercised the office of bishop during the Jerusalem Council. Some similarly point to Titus's oversight of a number of churches (Titus 1:7). Another argument sometimes put forward is that this model is not distinctly forbidden in the New Testament. However, the more important question is this: Is it *prescribed* in the Bible?

Presbyterian

In the Presbyterian model, churches are not ruled by bishops, but by elders. Some elders also have authority within the denomination regionally or even nationally.

"The local church is governed by the session, which is composed of ruling elders elected by the membership, with the teaching elder or minister as presiding officer."[6] Typically the congregation elects the ruling elders, or laymen, from the congregation, to serve as representatives of the members. Together the teaching elder and those ruling elders constitute the session and govern the local church.

"The next highest-ranking body is the Presbytery, which includes all the ordained ministers or teaching elders and one ruling elder from each local congregation in a given district. Above the presbytery is the synod, and over the synod is the general assembly, the highest court. Both of these bodies are also equally divided between ministers and laymen or ruling elders."[7]

The denominations that practice this form of government are primarily Presbyterians and various Reformed churches.

To defend this structure, some point to 1 Timothy 5:17, where Paul makes a distinction between elders who rule and those who teach. Some point to Paul's instruction to Titus (1:5) to ordain elders in every church, drawing the implication of regional or national oversight.

However, the Bible nowhere explicitly calls for elders to have or exercise authority beyond their own local flock. Some argue that Acts 15 is one possible exception, when the Jerusalem church elders sent an authoritative letter to other churches. But that passage cannot be used to defend Presbyterian government. After all, the apostles were still present and the ultimate authority behind that letter, and there are no apostles with such authority today. Also, the church in Antioch voluntarily requested the assistance of the Jerusalem church, likely because of the presence of the apostles. In addition, Acts 15:22 says that the *entire Jerusalem church* sent the letter to the other churches. In light of that, Wayne Grudem writes, "If this narrative gives support to regional government by elders, it therefore also gives support to regional government by whole congregations."[8]

Congregational

A third form of church government is congregational, where ultimate authority for each local church resides within each church—which is completely autonomous. The denominations that follow this form are

Congregational, Baptist, Mennonite, Evangelical Free, independent, and others. The congregational form of church government has a number of variations and expressions.

A very common congregational model is that of a single elder or pastor supported by a deacon board. Those who follow this approach often teach that 1 Timothy 3 prescribes a single elder in each church with a plurality of deacons, since the word *elder* is singular in that passage. However, the singular can also be used collectively as opposed to a single individual.

Another congregational structure is the corporate board model, in which the congregation chooses its pastor and also selects members to exercise oversight over the pastor (as CEO) and the entire organization, just like the board of a corporation.

Another form of congregationalism is pure democracy. Churches that practice this kind of government often seriously struggle with unity. My father-in-law pastored in the South for many years and once witnessed a serious breach in unity in a nearby "democratic" church. The contention centered on the color of shingles to use on the church's roof. The debate was so heated they decided the only way to keep the church from splitting was to put one color of shingles on half the roof and another color on the other half. Sadly, for years the members sat only under the half of the roof that had been shingled with their preferred color.

A Plurality of Elders

A final form of church government, and the model I will argue Scripture teaches, is that in every church there should be a plurality of godly men chosen by the elders and affirmed by the congregation. One of those elders usually serves as the primary pastor-teacher, the one delegated the chief responsibility to teach the Word to the flock.

Plurality in the Old Testament

The background for this type of church government is first found in the pattern of leadership in Old Testament Israel, which created a mind-set among the Jewish people who formed the earliest churches. There are two primary words translated "elder" in the Old Testament. The first is זָקֵן [*zaqen*], which means "old or mature in age." This word is usually found in the plural form and occurs 178 times in the Old Testament—about 100 of those occurrences refer to men in a position of authority. The other word is הָבִיְשׂ [siyb], an Aramaic word used five times in the post-exilic book of Ezra. This word means "gray-headed" and speaks of age and maturity.

When we examine how these two words are used in the Old Testament, we find the primary reference to elders occurs within the context of family: within the tribe, clan, and house or family. This usage is clear in Genesis 50:7: "Joseph went up to bury his father, and with him went up all the servants of Pharaoh, the elders of his household and all the elders of the land of Egypt." Second Samuel 12:17 tells us that "the elders of [David's] household stood beside him in order to raise him up from the ground, but he was unwilling and would not eat food with them [after his child died]." The elders of David's household sought to end his mourning and encourage him.

In the Old Testament, elders also ruled over cities administrating the local government. For example, in Ruth 4:1-2 we read, "Boaz went up to the gate and sat down there, and behold, the close relative of whom Boaz spoke was passing by, so he said, 'Turn aside, friend, sit down here.' And he turned aside and sat down. He took ten men of the elders of the city…" Within the family there were elders. And elders oversaw the life and government of the city (cf. Numbers 22:4, 7; Deuteronomy 19:12; 21:1ff, 19; 22:15; Judges 8:14).

There were also elders over nations—a plurality of men who served as leaders and advisors. This was common throughout the ancient world, even in the nations around Israel. For example, Numbers 22:7 refers to the elders of Moab and Genesis 50:7 to the elders of Egypt.

And the structure of elders over the nation was common in Israel and existed as early as the time of Moses. Exodus 4:29-30 tells us that in Egypt "Moses and Aaron went and assembled all the elders of the sons of Israel; and Aaron spoke all the words which the LORD had spoken to Moses." Before Moses officially began his ministry, there was already a body of men, the elders of Israel, to whom Moses presented what the Lord had spoken (cf. Exodus 3:16; 4:29; 12:21; 17:5; 18:12; 24:1, 9, 11, 14). In Numbers 11, Moses appointed 70 men to assist in leading the people of Israel. Some

Jewish scholars point to that event as the beginning of the Sanhedrin—the 70 elders of Israel, as they referred to them.

This group of elders continued to serve as an advisory body during the monarchy (1 Samuel 8:4; 2 Samuel 3:17; 5:3; 17:4, 15; 19:11; 1 Kings 20:7; 21:8; 23:1). Even though there was a king on the throne and there were prophets to keep the king in check, Israel still had this body of elders, which continued even into the New Testament era. Elders were also influential during the exile in Babylon. According to Ezekiel 8:1, the elders continued to wield considerable influence (cf. Jeremiah 29:1; 14:1; 20:1). After the return from exile, they were called on a number of occasions to help mediate specific problems and issues (Ezra 5:9ff; 6:7; 10:8, 14). And, of course, in the Gospels we find many references to the elders of Israel functioning as the Sanhedrin and highest ruling body of Judaism.

Clearly, in the first-century Jewish mind, the word *elders* referred to a plurality of godly leaders. With that history, it was natural for the concept of elder rule to be adopted by the first churches, which were primarily Jewish and under the responsibility and leadership of the apostles.

Plurality in the New Testament

In addition to the Old Testament pattern, the New Testament and the apostolic example provide overwhelming evidence for a plurality of godly men leading each church.

Elders played a dominant role in the life of the church in Jerusalem and at the Jerusalem Council. Throughout the book of Acts, Luke refers to the church in the singular but to elders in the plural form. Each church had a plurality of elders. That pattern permeates the New Testament.

For example, in Acts 15:4 we read, "When they arrived in Jerusalem, they were received by the church [singular] and the apostles and the elders [plural], and they reported all that God had done with them." Notice that same pattern appears in verse 22: "It seemed good to the apostles and the elders [plural], with the whole church [singular], to choose men from among them to send to Antioch with Paul and Barnabas" (cf. Acts 11:30; 15:2, 6, 23; 16:4; 21:18).

James was written to Jewish believers dispersed because of persecution—probably the persecution of Herod mentioned in Acts 12. Written in the mid-40s AD, it may have been the first New Testament book written, so the formation of the church would have been at an early stage. James wrote to small groups of believers dispersed across Eastern Europe, and yet there is already a pattern of multiple elders within each church. In James 5:14, he writes, "Is anyone among you sick? Then he must call for the elders [plural] of the church [singular] and they are to pray over him, anointing him with oil in the name of the Lord."

Acts 14 is a crucial passage because it contains the first mention of elders in a *Gentile* congregation, near the end of Paul's first missionary journey. In verse 23, Luke writes: "When they had appointed elders [plural] for them in every church [singular], having prayed with fasting, they commended them to the Lord in whom they had believed." Luke uses the Greek preposition *kata* in a distributive sense: "having appointed for them church by church, elders." He is referring to the churches in Antioch of Pisidia, Iconium, Lystra, and Derbe. So one of the key steps in organizing a new church was appointing elders. This was Paul's pattern everywhere he went.

In Acts 20, Paul concluded his third missionary journey and headed to Jerusalem for the Feast of Pentecost, around May AD 57. Earlier on that same journey, Paul had established the church in Ephesus and ministered there for about three years. On his way to Jerusalem, Paul's ship docked in Miletus for several days to load and unload cargo. Miletus was only 40 miles south of Ephesus, so Paul seized the opportunity to summon the Ephesian elders with whom he had ministered for three years. His words in Acts 20 are the only record of Paul speaking directly to a group of elders in the entire New Testament. Verse 17 says that "from Miletus he sent to Ephesus and called to him the elders [plural] of the church [singular]." In verse 28, Paul warned these elders, "Be on guard for yourselves and for all the flock, among which the Holy Spirit has made you [plural] overseers." There was one flock, and these elders were responsible to oversee it. The church in Ephesus had a plurality of godly men who led and pastored it. Timothy also later ministered in Ephesus. In 1 Timothy 5:17, we discover that there were still multiple elders in that church.

Philippians 1:1 was written later in Paul's ministry. He wrote "to all the saints in Christ Jesus who are in Philippi, including the overseers and deacons." At that point, the church in Philippi was more than ten years old.

Paul was under house arrest in Rome, and this church with its heart for the apostle had sent him an offering and had also sent Epaphroditus to minister to him. In his response (the letter to the Philippians), the apostle identified two offices in this church: the office of overseer, and the office of deacon. Both are mentioned in the plural form, and we know there was only one body of believers, one church in Philippi. Fifty years later, Polycarp wrote to the Philippian church: "to the Church of God which sojourns at Philippi." He called the church (singular) to submit to its deacons and elders (plural).[9]

According to Acts 27:7, the ship taking Paul to Rome had taken shelter on the south side of Crete. And after release from his first Roman imprisonment, he visited Crete. By the time Paul wrote Titus, his son in the faith, the churches on Crete were probably already established. But they were weak, having been assaulted by false teachers (Titus 1:10-16; 3:9-11). Because of that relentless assault, Paul left Titus there for a specific purpose: "For this reason I left you in Crete, that you would set in order what remains and appoint elders [plural] in every city [singular]" (Titus 1:5). Since Crete is a small island with small cities, it is likely there was only one church in each city, and elders—plural—were to be appointed in each of those churches.

A Leader Among Leaders

Whenever the word *elder* is connected to the word *church* in the New Testament, we find a singular flock overseen by a plural number of elders. That pattern is consistent even with our Lord and His ministry. He gave the early church a plurality of leaders: He appointed 12 apostles. Then He sent the 12 out two by two, with equal rank and authority. But obviously even among the apostles there were leaders among leaders. In Scripture, the apostles are always listed in three groups of four. The same men are always in the same group of four. And the first name in each group is always the same—apparently there was a leader of each group. And Peter's name is always mentioned first. So even the apostles illustrate the principle of a plurality of leaders and of leaders among leaders by virtue of experience, age, and skills. Christ ordained the basic concept of plurality even with the apostles.

Elder, Overseer, and Shepherd

Both the Old and New Testaments provide ample evidence for the concept of a plurality of elders in the church, but there is one more important line of argument based on the Greek words that describe the office of elder. These words not only help us understand the number of elders required but also their duties.

First, the Greek word translated "elder" is *presbyteros*. It has two primary uses in the New Testament. One use is to describe older men. For example, 1 Timothy 5:1 tells us not to rebuke an older man, but to appeal to him as a father. This word is also used as a title for a community official. There is no specific age demanded by this word, but it does imply maturity, dignity, experience, and honor. When the Bible connects a particular age to the commencement of spiritual leadership, the examples point to about thirty years of age. For example, a man who belonged to the descendants of Aaron could enter full service in the priesthood at 30 (Numbers 4:46-47). Our Lord began His earthly ministry at about that age as well (Luke 3:23). Many commentators believe Timothy was in his early thirties (1 Timothy 4:12). Although those examples of age are not binding on the office of elder in the local church, they can help provide a general guideline.

The same word is used 28 times in the Gospels and Acts to refer to the Sanhedrin. It is used 12 times in Revelation to describe the 24 elders who are representatives of the redeemed in heaven. It is also used 19 times in Acts and the epistles to refer to a group of leaders in each church.

The second Greek word, *episkopos*, is translated "overseer" and in some versions, "bishop." The word was commonly used to refer to secular officials of various kinds, especially local officials such as superintendents, managers, controllers, and rulers.

The Septuagint uses this word of military officers (Numbers 31:14), tabernacle administrators (Numbers 4:16), supervisors of temple repair (2 Chronicles 24:12, 17), temple guardians (2 Kings 11:18), city supervisors, and mayors (Nehemiah 11:9). It appears only five times in the New Testament. Once it is used of Christ (1 Peter 2:25) and the other four times of church leaders, especially in the context of Gentile congregations like that in Ephesus. It is a general word like *supervisor, manager,* or *guardian.*

It is necessary to examine multiple passages that address this concept of managing and supervising to develop a clear picture of the responsibility of elders. In 1 Timothy 5:17, Paul wrote, "The elders who rule well are to be considered worthy of double honor, especially those who work hard at preaching and teaching." The Greek word translated "rule" [*proistēmi*] means "to set over, to rule." It is also translated several other ways in the New Testament. For example, it is translated "leads" in Romans 12:8 in reference to the gift of administration. It is translated "manage" in 1 Timothy 3:4-5 in reference to an elder's oversight of his household. It is translated "managers" in 1 Timothy 3:12 in reference to deacons managing their children and their households.

While all elders are to be able to teach, some elders labor at preaching and teaching (1 Timothy 5:17). Paul implies that some elders have greater teaching responsibilities, probably because of superior giftedness. But all the elders are to manage everything that happens in their local church. That does not mean that they must do all the work, but they must ensure everything is done decently and in order.

A third Greek word, *poimēn*, translates as "shepherd" or "pastor." The *noun* form occurs 18 times in the New Testament—of shepherds that keep animals, of Christ (e.g., Hebrews 13:20-21; 1 Peter 2:25), and once of church leaders. The *verb* form, used three times in the context of church leaders, emphasizes the pastor's primary role—teaching or leading his sheep. In John 21:16, Christ commanded Peter, "Shepherd My sheep." In Acts 20:28, Paul reminded the Ephesian elders that they were to *shepherd* the church of God. And in 1 Peter 5:1-2, Peter charged the elders scattered across Asia Minor to shepherd the flock of God.

All three words—*elder*, *overseer*, and *shepherd*—clearly refer to the same office. The qualifications for an *overseer* in 1 Timothy 3 and an *elder* in Titus 1 are almost identical. Also, Paul told Titus to appoint elders (1:5) and then called the same men *overseers* (1:7). First Peter 5:1-2 brings all three words and concepts together into one office: "I exhort the elders among you, as your fellow *elder*...[to] *shepherd* the flock of God among you, exercising *oversight*" (emphasis added).

Paul also uses these three terms interchangeably in Acts 20:17, 28: "From Miletus he sent to Ephesus and called to him the *elders* of the church...Be on guard for yourselves and for all the flock, among which the Holy Spirit has made you *overseers*, to *shepherd* the church of God" (emphasis added).

Together these three terms describe the office: *elder* emphasizes the man's character—his spiritual maturity. *Shepherd* and *overseer* refer to his function. A *shepherd* feeds, protects, and cares for his people. An *overseer* rules or has charge over both the people and the ministry of the church. So *elder*, *shepherd*, and *overseer* all identify the same person, serving in the same office. But the New Testament pattern is a group of qualified elders leading every local church.

Required Today?

One final question must be answered: Is this clear biblical pattern a mandate for churches today? For all who take the New Testament and the pastoral epistles seriously, it must be! The pastoral epistles were written to church leaders to dictate how they are to conduct themselves in the household of God (1 Timothy 3:15). Within these books, Paul insists on a plurality of leadership (cf. 1 Timothy 5:17; Titus 1:5). In addition, there is the weight of apostolic example. The apostles probably established elder rule in the Jewish churches (Acts 15:6). That is why James, who ministered alongside the apostles in Jerusalem and was the most influential leader in the Jerusalem church, expected elder rule in the Diaspora (James 5:14). Paul established elder rule in all the Gentile churches (Acts 14:23) and commanded Titus to appoint elders in every church as well (Titus 1:5). So this form of church government carries apostolic authority and has been prescribed for all church leaders with all the weight of inspired Scripture.

If a plurality of godly elders already leads your church, this should serve as a great encouragement. If not, carefully study what Scripture teaches about this topic. If you conclude that your church government needs to change, pray for wisdom and move very slowly.

The first step toward change is to establish the sufficiency and authority of Scripture. Remind your congregation that whatever Scripture says about any issue must be obeyed and followed, even if it requires difficult changes. Then begin slowly over time to teach the biblical pattern of church leadership. In the meantime, identify a few men who meet the qualifications for elders and begin to rely on them for help and counsel, even though they do not yet carry that title. Have them begin to function as elders, even if they do not yet occupy the office per se. It may take years but work toward the goal of your congregation embracing the biblical pattern. It will take time. Do not try to change your church to elder rule quickly. But do make moving in that direction a priority, because the Old Testament pattern, the New Testament evidence, and the Greek words for the pastoral office combine to form an unbreakable chain of evidence. God intends that a local church be governed by a plurality of godly men. Therefore, it is to that pattern that every biblical church must aspire.

PRAYER

Father, we are overwhelmed by the grace You have shown us in Christ. We thank You, from the bottom of our hearts, that we stand righteous before You, wearing not a righteousness of our own, but a righteousness that comes to us from Jesus Christ. Father, we are further overwhelmed that not only have You given us the great privilege of belonging to You, but You have given us the incredible responsibility and opportunity to serve in Your body. We ask that You will make us faithful stewards of that calling. We pray these things in Jesus' name. Amen.

THE GREAT COMMISSION AS A THEOLOGICAL ENDEAVOR

"Go therefore and make disciples of all the nations,
baptizing them in the name of the Father
and the Son and the Holy Spirit,
teaching them to observe all that I commanded you."

MATTHEW 28:19-20

9

THE GREAT COMMISSION AS A THEOLOGICAL ENDEAVOR

Paul Washer

Shepherds' Conference 2014

Matthew 28:16-20

The eleven disciples proceeded to Galilee, to the mountain which Jesus had designated. When they saw Him, they worshiped Him; but some were doubtful. And Jesus came and spoke to them, saying, "All authority has been given to Me in heaven and on earth. Go therefore and make disciples of all the nations, baptizing them in the name of the Father and the Son and the Holy Spirit, teaching them to observe all that I commanded you; and lo, I am with you always, even to the end of the age" (Matthew 28:16-20).

There are four things in particular to note from this passage. First, we see a reflection of our weakness. Second, we see a declaration of Christ—His absolute authority and power. Third, we see the preeminent task of the church. Fourth, if all this is too much, if it overwhelms us, we have the promise of His presence and power. For every man who has taken the Great Commission seriously, this last promise is the thing that holds him. It is what strengthens him and makes him go on.

Our Weakness

Let's look first at a reflection of our weakness. Verses 16 and 17 read, "The eleven disciples proceeded to Galilee, to the mountain which Jesus had designated. When they saw Him, they worshiped Him; but some were doubtful." Here we do not see great men of faith. Instead, we see men like us—a mixture of faith and obedience, doubt and uncertainty. The Greek word that is used here for doubt is *distzo*, meaning "a double standing." That is to say, there was an uncertainty or a hesitancy about them. It is the same word that was used to describe Peter when he was commanded by Christ to come out of the boat and walk upon the raging sea.

Now, I want to be fair at this moment to these men. We should not just attribute this doubt to their weakness, but also to the magnitude of what they were being called to believe and do. Let's think for a moment about Peter being called to walk out onto the Sea of Galilee, and yet that was nothing compared to what they were being called to do at this very moment.

These men were being called to walk out into the sea of humanity— a radically depraved humanity. They were being sent out as lambs in the midst of wolves. They were being called to cast down every earthly power and authority, to do so by faith and by the proclamation of the most scandalous message that the world has ever known, which was first spoken by a carpenter. We can see that there is at least something of a reason for their doubt.

One of the greatest things I have ever learned from Scripture regarding the apostles is that they were like us. But we see here that they would be transformed to become something more than mere men. How would that happen? They grasped, by the power and ministry of the Holy Spirit, the reality of the absolute authority of Jesus Christ, as is evident in the book of Acts.

When we talk about missions and those who participate in missions, there are at least three qualifications that are absolute essentials. First, we need men who are constantly growing in their knowledge of the person and work of Christ—who He truly is and what He has truly done. Second, we need men who will renounce once and for all every fleshly means of planting churches and doing missions. And third, we need men who are constantly, unceasingly crying out for greater manifestations of the life and power of the Holy Spirit in their own life.

Just because there are so many wrong men teaching so many wrong things about the Holy Spirit doesn't mean we should overreact against them and turn our Trinity into something less than it is. Do not allow false prophets to rob you of your inheritance of the Spirit. We cannot fulfill the Great Commission apart from the power, the teaching, the righteousness, the holiness, and the life of the Holy Spirit.

Declaration of His Power

Having looked at the reflection of our weakness, let's see now the declaration of His power. Verse 18 reads, "Jesus came up and spoke to them, saying, 'All authority has been given to Me in heaven and on earth.'" Jesus knows their weakness, and He goes out to meet them. How many times in your ministry has this been true? He knew your weakness at that moment, but He did not leave you. Instead, He went out to meet you—He came for you. What a blessed Savior, what a broad-shouldered God we have. He knows our frame. He knows that we are dust. There has never been a great man of God, nor will there ever be; only tiny little faithless men of a great and a merciful God. He went out to meet them.

A young person came to me and said, "But the Great Commission is so great and I'm so weak." My response was, "Yes, but as someone once wrote, 'Christ does not call men who are worthy. Christ makes men worthy by virtue of the calling.'"

What exactly did Christ do here? He came out and He countered the disciples' doubt and uncertainty. He did so with a declaration of His absolute authority over everything, without limitation, jurisdiction, or exception. This is His power.

David Brown, a well-known Scottish theologian and exegete, said, "What must have been the feelings which such a Commission awakened? We who have scarce conquered our own misgivings—we, fishermen of Galilee, with no letters, no means, no influence over the humblest creature, conquer the world for Thee, Lord? Nay, Lord, do not mock us.'"[1]

The Lord did not mock. He responded, "All authority has been given to

Me in heaven and on earth. Go therefore…and lo, I am with you always, even to the end of the age" (verses 18-20).

Our strength—our everything—is not found in us; it is all found in Him. A wonderful illustration of Christ's authority is found in Genesis 41:44: "Pharaoh said to Joseph, 'Though I am Pharaoh, yet without your permission no one shall raise his hand or foot in all the land of Egypt.'" The resurrected and exalted Christ stands before the Father, and all authority is given to Him in heaven and on earth. It is as though the Father said to the Son, "Without Your permission, Son, no one will raise his hand or his foot in all the cosmos."

Even the hand that was raised to throw the first stone at Stephen was under the sovereign jurisdiction of the Lord Jesus Christ. Knowing this is what will make a weak man strong. What does this kind of authority mean for our missionary endeavors? It means that he who goes to and fro weeping, carrying his bag of seeds, will come again with a shout of joy, bringing his seeds with him. Is this authority just some theological speculation, something to be talked about in a seminary? Absolutely not! It is essential for everything we do in world missions. His authority means that there will be a great multitude which no one can count standing before the throne and the Lamb. They will be clothed in white robes, and each one will have in his hand a palm branch, and they will cry out with a great and unified voice, "Salvation to our God who sits on the throne, and to the Lamb" (Revelation 7:10). His authority means we will win, because He has won. What an open door lies before us, and what strength He has given us in His name.

Most people involved in missions would give a hearty amen to everything I have said thus far. Jesus is Lord, and He has authority and power. But we must understand the implications of the sovereignty of Christ. If we are to go out *in* His authority, then we must go out *under* His authority. That means everything we do in missions and church planting, everything that we believe, everything that we practice, and all of our so-called strategies and methodologies must all be warranted by the Scriptures, or we have no authority at all. Our authority comes from our conformity to what this mighty Lord has commanded.

I believe the Achilles' heel of modern evangelical missions is that everyone is doing what is right in their own eyes. Our missions methodology and our church-planting strategies are not to be the invention of the anthropologist, the sociologist, or the expert in leading cultural trends. Then from where should our strategy and our methodology come? It should come from the Scriptures, drawn out of the Scriptures by the exegete, the theologian, and the church historian. But these have been all but removed from modern evangelical missions. That is our Achilles' heel.

I'm reminded of Moses being told to make everything in the tabernacle according to the pattern that was shown to him on the mountain. Now if God can say that about the tabernacle, how much more the greatest of all causes. See to it that you do this Great Commission according to the pattern that has been shown in the Holy Scriptures.

God has given the church and her ministers the Scriptures so that we might be equipped not for some good works, not for certain good words, but for every necessary work of the kingdom. God has also given the Scriptures to the church so that we might know how to conduct ourselves in the household of God—the church of the living God, the pillar and the support of the truth.

The Reformation, the Puritans, Spurgeon, Calvin, Lloyd-Jones—none of them were wrapped up in Calvinism. They were wrapped up in the sufficiency of Scripture. Of course part of that is a right understanding of soteriology. But all over America, I see men who are supposedly going back to the truth, but only with regard to soteriology. If I look at their church planting and their way of doing missions, it looks just like every other evangelical. It is not just about reforming your soteriology, for the Puritan genius was this: They sought to take every aspect of life and ministry, and submit it to a book, the Scriptures. Yet there is this prevalent idea of taking the Puritans, and the Reformers, and dressing all of it up to fit the culture so that other people today will appreciate it. We must cling to what is written, and we must do our church planting, our church life, our missions, our families, and everything else according to what is written and not what is right in our own eyes.

Someone came to me and said, "Brother Paul, I believe in the inerrancy of Scripture." I replied, "Good for you, because the inerrancy of Scripture means nothing unless you also practice the sufficiency of Scripture."

They are twin sisters. Inerrancy—you can hold onto that without being changed—but to take that doctrine and move on to sufficiency, now that is a whole other ball game.

If we are going to fulfill the Great Commission, we must lay aside every fleshly strategy and methodology. We must go into the Scriptures and follow the pattern that is given to us there. The more we, as a people, hold on to the works, strategies, and methodologies of the flesh, the less that we will see God. What must we do? We must rip from us—like a poison, like a plague, like a scab—Saul's armor, and we must go out and pick up the smooth stones of the gospel that for too long have been neglected. Beloved, that is the only way we are ever going to go out and slay this Goliath called world missions.

The Church's Preeminent Task

Let us now look at what specifically the church is called to do. Matthew 28:19-20 reads, "Go therefore and make disciples of all the nations, baptizing them in the name of the Father and the Son and the Holy Spirit, teaching them to observe all that I commanded you; and lo, I am with you always, even to the end of the age." Please note that I call this point the church's preeminent task and not the church's preeminent command. The church's preeminent command is to love the Lord your God with all your heart, soul, mind, and strength. The second command is to love your neighbor as yourself. Only men who have been changed through the regenerating work of the Holy Spirit and the renewal of their mind in the Scriptures can have a love for God that propels them to do great things in God's name.

A Labor of Love

The Great Commission is a labor of love. We love God, and therefore we desire that the knowledge of the glory of God be upon this earth like the waters that cover the sea. We desire that the name of God be great among the nations, from the rising to the setting of the sun. We love Christ, and therefore we desire that the Lamb receive the full reward of His suffering. We love men—and if you don't love men then you need to get out of ministry—and we cannot tolerate their suffering; therefore, we want to see God glorified in their salvation. It is a labor of love.

We must remain under His authority, and He commands us to love Him and our neighbor. We must constantly, daily, not only in our public life, nor only in our pulpit ministry, but also in our private life, remain under His authority. He bought you, He owns you, and you are not your own, so take that truth and drive it like a stake straight through the heart of the flesh. You are His!

Young men, if you have not settled that matter before you graduate, all the degrees in the world will not help you. We go out in His name because we love Him. We love Him because He first loved us. When you go and preach on the street and the people listening turn on you after about five minutes—they grab your little pulpit, megaphone, all your tracts and Bibles, and even you and throw it all off the plaza into the street—it is going to take a lot more than simple love for people for you to pick up everything and march right back to that plaza again. For that kind of persistence and endurance to exist, it is going to take the love of Christ manifested in your life—the reality of what He has done for you. Although your suffering might not be that dramatic, it is oftentimes more intense. In order for you to keep going, serving, blessing, though unnoticed and unappreciated by men, it is going to take this standard and comprehension of the reality of Christ.

Make Disciples

Jesus then said to His followers, "Make disciples" (verse 19). The phrase "make disciples" has the prominent idea of instruction and teaching. Making disciples is the means of communicating truth. What is a disciple? It is someone who is like his master. So the end of church planting and the end of the Great Commission is not recording decisions or counting converts; it is taking the gospel of Jesus Christ and boldly proclaiming it to the lost. And when those lost are soundly converted, then we enter into a lifelong labor with the full counsel of God's Word for their sanctification. That is what we are called to do.

Now this is difficult work. You will leave this wonderful, necessary, and edifying conference and go back to this difficult task. But the hard work pays off, for I would take one sound disciple over 10,000 so-called converts that evangelicalism is producing today. The idea of making disciples is further clarified by Paul in his letter to Timothy: "The things which you have heard from me in the presence of many witnesses, entrust these to faithful men who will be able to teach others also" (2 Timothy 2:2). This text is so often used out of context by individuals who reference it to stress that the moment someone is converted they need to go and disciple someone else who has been converted more recently. That type of discipleship has its place, but that is not what Paul is talking about here. Paul is telling Timothy to raise up leaders, to raise up men of God, and to raise up men who are qualified to be elders and biblical deacons.

We are called to make disciples even when the circumstances are not ideal. It is amazing that Jesus never said, "The harvest is great, but the money is few." Money is not the problem. Men of integrity—biblical men who have lashed themselves down to Scripture—that is the rarity. Christians who are making disciples is the gem, and we are called to this task. Although these kinds of men are being produced at The Master's Seminary and at other good seminaries that the Lord has raised up, never forget that this work is the primary task of the church.

Jesus then said that this work is to be done in all nations. If you have had a measure of success in the ministry and you are content, then it shows that you have a very small, shriveled heart. There is a sense in which the man of God who has been obedient, regardless of so-called success, is able to lay his head down at night and sleep. However, we should not be content just because we have had some measure of success in our little fishbowl. We should not be content until the name of Jesus Christ is proclaimed to every person of our generation, until His flag flies on every hill, mountain, and valley. We can be content when His name is glorified on every inch of this planet.

There has never been a time in the history of the world when an effectual door has been as opened as it is now. I'm not a prophet nor the son of a prophet, but through studying church history, human history, and secular history, I would tell you that a shadow is growing in the West. I don't know how long we will have this privilege to go out to all the nations, for it could be very soon that we are running for our lives. So while it is day let us work, for night comes when no man labors.

I used to write all the time in the back of our magazine, "Just what part of 'go' do you not understand?"[2] Then I realized that with regard to the evangelical community, the answer is that most individuals don't understand "go." Now you all know that "go" is not the primary command in the passage—"make disciples" is. Craig Blomberg, in his commentary on Matthew, gives this helpful insight: "Too much and too little have often been made of this observation."[3] It is emphasized too much when a church or a minister thinks that they are called to bloom only where they are planted—that they are doing the work because they are doing ministry in their Jerusalem. They are not granted that luxury because though they must minister in Jerusalem, they cannot forget the nations.

Also, too much emphasis is placed on "go" and not enough on "make disciples." This is the great sin of evangelicalism today, when we frantically give in to blatant pragmatism. When we look at the need of the world, too often we act in a way that is not biblical—that is, by sending people into the mission field who should not be on the mission field. This means individuals who do not meet the requirements set forth in Titus 1 and 1 Timothy 3. We cannot keep sending young, untrained people who do not even understand the word *propitiation* to the mission field. We must send qualified men, for this is an absolute necessity.

Another way in which we emphasize "go" too much is when we succumb to the carnal strategies that are being put before men today with regard to how to do missions and how to plant churches. These strategies are absurd. They are made by little boys who know nothing of the power of God, who know nothing about intercessory prayer, and who do not believe in the power of proclamation. We need to lay aside these strategies once and for all, and use what the Scriptures give us to use.

The missionary enterprise is actually quite simple. You can divide it up into two ministries. You are either called to go, or you are called to send those who are going. Either way, the same devotion is required. William Carey told men, "I will go down [in the mine that is India], if you will hold the rope."[4] Missions is either you go down the rope into the mine, or you hold the rope for those who go down. Either way, there will be scars on your hands and exhaustion on your faces. Where are your scars? Where are the scars of your church? Where is the exhaustion? Where is the labor?

Pastors can be the greatest catalyst or the greatest hindrance when it comes to involving people in sacrificing for missions. The church is looking at their pastor. Is he concerned for the Indonesians who do not know the gospel? Is he concerned for countless good men, genuinely converted, trying to labor in some jungle somewhere, but do not have a clue how to interpret the Scriptures because they have not had the privileges you have? You must involve your people in missions. You must go, or you must send.

We live in an age of media, cyberspace, computers, Internet, and technology, and I praise God for that because we are able to send books, literature, and other things into closed countries. But we cannot fulfill the Great Commission online. It must be through incarnational missions. When God decided to send the gospel, He became a man and dwelt among us, and He is calling the church to do the same—to send flesh and blood. There should be no reason why we do not have missionaries all over the world. There should never be a reason why a missionary is walking around beggarly, trying to find a few books or raise a little money. Where is our faith, and where is our boldness?

I embrace fully the Westminster Confession and the 1689 London Confession with regard to their statements concerning the sovereignty of God. But sometimes I pray, "God, what do You want me to do in this situation?" Now, I don't hear a voice in response, but often this thought comes into my head: *Well, what can you believe Me for? How far do you want to take this?*

Just how big is your God? I'm so tired of men hiding behind the sovereignty of God. It is not a catalyst to permit us to remain passive; it is a catalyst to compel us to fight. I do not need a lightbulb to explode in my study while I'm praying to know that the gospel needs to be preached more in Indonesia. He has said, "Go, and to every nation, but go properly."

Baptize Them

Jesus also said that as we make disciples we are to baptize them. There are a few things to mention concerning this. First, our converts must accept the full and unique Christian teaching. The text mentions baptizing in the very specific name of the Father, the Son, and the Holy Spirit. The God of the Bible is not the God of the Koran. The God of the Bible is not just like all other gods with a different name. The God of the Bible is not merely optional among many other religious options. He is the Name, the Way, the Truth, and the Life. You and I can end the 2000-year war between the secular world and the church by just changing an article—from a definite article to an indefinite article. All we have to do to be the toast of the secular world is to say that we believe in Jesus and that He is *a* way, *a* truth, and *a* life. But if we say that, we destroy the power of the gospel and we damn our own souls. There is no other name.

Also, our converts must publicly profess Jesus Christ as Lord. So many missionaries respond to me, "But if they do that they'll suffer." I don't say this lightly—yes, they will. I'm not saying we should lay aside all wisdom, that we should go out and try to be persecuted, or that we should demand these things from brothers in persecuted countries. But missions and suffering go hand in hand. Much of the missionary strategy today is designed so that missionaries and their converts do not have to suffer, but suffering is a part of representing Jesus Christ. In many of the countries with the greatest persecution of Christians, if you go home and tell everybody you believe in Jesus, they won't have a problem with it, even in some Muslim countries. It is when you identify with Jesus Christ and His church, through baptism, and renounce all other religions, gods, and doctrines—that is when all hell breaks loose. Converts must identify with Christ publicly. The apostles never sought to teach people how to avoid suffering. Rather, they predicted suffering, and were determined to prepare people for it.

The last thing to say about baptism is that we are not called to leave in our wake a bunch of disconnected individual disciples. We are called to bring those disciples together in a church. Not a Bible study, not a worship group, but a church. And we are to labor until that church has a mature leadership, mature doctrine, is autonomous, strong, and biblical. Lately, missionaries have been trying to build culturally sensitive churches instead of biblically faithful churches. We should not take Western culture and force it on another culture. We should challenge the West and its culture, and when we go into other cultures, we must do the same. The standard that challenges culture is the Word of God.

The Great Commission is didactic. It is a theological endeavor. It is not about sending missionaries per se; it is about sending the truth through missionaries—to teach all to observe the truth. The Great Commission is not just about *gnosis*, it is about *praxis*; it is not just about orthodoxy, it is about orthopraxy. This is very clear in the teaching of Christ when He says, "Take My yoke upon you and learn from Me" (Matthew 11:29). The two always go hand in hand. To learn from Him is to submit to His sovereignty.

Teach Them

Then Jesus said in the Great Commission that we are to be "teaching them to observe all that I commanded you." What is the source? From where are we to teach people? What is to be our source of information? To teach them "all that I commanded you" (verse 20). We teach the words of Christ, the Word of the living God. Missions is not about sending missionaries; it is about sending God's truth through missionaries. I mention this simple statement again because we have more missionary activity today than at probably any other time in history, and yet most of it is smoke and mirrors. Dust! And when it all settles, I do not know how much truth will remain.

Because we are sending truth, the missionary must be an exegete. He must be a theologian. He must be both a proclaimer and a scribe. One of the best illustrations of a missionary, even though to his own people, was Ezra, for he set his heart to study the law of God, to practice it, and to teach its statutes and ordinances in Israel (Ezra 7:10). That is a missionary.

A young man contacted me years ago while I was in Peru and said, "I want to come down there, brother Paul, and I want to work with you." I replied, "Well, talk to me about your time in the Word, talk to me about your knowledge, your study of the Scriptures." He said, "That's not my area. I just want to come down there and give my life away." I responded, "Well, then talk to me about intercessory prayer." He said, "That's really not my area. Brother Paul, I just want to come down there and give my life away." I did take the young man under my wing, but this is what I said to him, "Nobody in Peru needs your life. They need someone who can come here, open his mouth, and proclaim to them the Word of the living God. They need the life, death, and resurrection of Jesus taught to them."

The command to make disciples through teaching proves that the Great Commission is a theological and doctrinal endeavor. But if we look at the great majority of missionary work in the world today, we see that doctrine does not have a high priority—although at one time it was the queen of all sciences. Lacking theology, mission work today in many cases has become a glaring contradiction, even an absurdity.

There are a few ways in which that's going on. Number one, it has become the popular opinion that Christians should lay aside their doctrine and rally around a common confession of Jesus. There is only one problem: There are multiple Christs being preached in the world today, not only in so-called Christendom, but even in the realm of evangelicalism. Are we to preach a Christ that is so vague and so general that we tell the world to follow an undefined Jesus and contradictory opinions with regard to His Word? Absolutely not!

Number two—and this may be the most absurd thing that was ever birthed in the mind of a man—we need to lay aside our doctrine and rally around the Great Commission. However, since we have already come to the conclusion that the Great Commission is a doctrinal or theological endeavor, to lay aside doctrine and theology while fulfilling the Great Commission is suicide. This is the problem today, and it is the same problem for every generation of the church—a depreciation of truth. Yet Christianity is a truth religion, and the Great Commission is about the proclamation of the truth.

If you want to be an ivory-tower theologian who sits and pontificates and meditates, then you can have all kinds of undefined doctrine. If you want to be a seminary student who just argues theology in the student center, you can have all kinds of undefined doctrine. But when you go to plant a church and you are dealing with real people with real problems, defining the small stuff becomes very important. It is the common practice of missionary organizations to reduce their doctrinal statement down to the lowest common denominator so that they can bring in more candidates for the mission field and more supporters for those candidates. In many cases that is done by men with a desire to do something right. But it is a blatant surrender to pragmatism, and in the end, we lose our soul.

His Presence and Power

Jesus concludes the commission with these words: "Lo, I am with you always, even to the end of the age" (Matthew 28:20). The first word in that sentence communicates the idea of looking, seeing, beholding, taking notice. It is as though Christ was looking at these men and saying, "Look at Me! Look at Me! I am now going to give you the greatest of all encouragements. I will be with you always, even into the end of the age."

By these words, as I have previously suggested, Christ shows that in sending the apostles, He does not entirely resign His office as if He ceased to be the teacher of His church. For He sends away the apostles with this reservation: that they will not bring forward their own inventions, but will purely and faithfully deliver from hand to hand, as we say, what Jesus entrusted to them. That is the word of missions—to faithfully deliver to our hearers what has been entrusted to us. God will bless that kind of work in the mission field.

Why Every Self-Respecting Calvinist Must Be a Premillennialist

"For the gifts and calling of God are irrevocable."

Romans 11:29

10

WHY EVERY SELF–RESPECTING CALVINIST MUST BE A PREMILLENNIALIST

John MacArthur

Shepherds' Conference 2007

Selected Scriptures

I have a heartfelt concern for an area of theology that needs more careful attention than it has been given. The topic is sovereign election, Israel, and eschatology. One of the strange ironies in the church and in Reformed theology is that those who are most in love with the doctrine of sovereign election, who are most unwavering in their devotion to the glory of God, the honor of Christ, the work of the Spirit in regeneration and sanctification, who are adamant about the veracity and inerrancy of Scripture, who are fastidious in hermeneutics, who are the most careful when it comes to doctrine, who are guardians of biblical truth, and who are laboring with all their powers to determine the true interpretation of every text in divine revelation, yet at the same time are disinterested in applying those passions and skills to determining the end of the story, and are rather content to be in playful disagreement to the vast biblical data on eschatology.

Does Eschatology Matter?

Does the end matter to God, and should it matter to us? The culmination of all redemptive history is important. History is headed to a divinely designed conclusion, and it is significant enough that God has revealed it to us. God filled the Scriptures with end-time prophecies, and it has been estimated that nearly a quarter of the Bible, at the time it was written, relates to the eschaton.

Did God in this significant volume of revelation somehow muddle His words so hopelessly that the high ground for theologians is simply to recognize the muddle and abandon any thoughts of the perspicuity of Scripture with regard to eschatology? Is in fact working hard to understand prophetic passages needless and impossible because they require a spiritualized or allegorized set of interpretations? Are you comfortable with the notion that the tried-and-true principles of interpretation have to be set aside every time you come to a prophetic text?

Reclaiming a Literal Interpretation

There are a number of amillennialists and postmillennialists who state that many prophetic passages require a spiritualized or allegorized interpretation. The common view held by these two camps is that the kingdom promised to Israel, as identified in the Old Testament, was never meant to be fulfilled in a literal sense. O.T. Allis, a well-known amillennialist, acknowledges that a simple and literal interpretation of these Old Testament prophecies would require that the promises to Israel be realized by national Israel: "The Old Testament prophecies if literally interpreted, cannot be regarded as having been yet fulfilled or being capable of fulfillment in the present age."[1]

Floyd Hamilton, in *The Basis of Millennial Faith*, elaborates: "Now we must frankly admit that a literal interpretation of the Old Testament prophecies gives us just such a picture of an earthly reign of the Messiah as the pre-millennialist pictures."[2] Lorraine Boettner wrote, "In the meaning of the Millennium, it is generally agreed that if the prophecies are taken literally, they do foretell a restoration of the nation of Israel in the land of Palestine, with the Jews having a prominent place in that kingdom and ruling over the other nations."[3]

All three of these cases required a severe alteration in hermeneutics in order to avoid a premillennial conclusion, which apparently, in their view, is a fate worse than death. To protect some kind of preconceived theological position, it is necessary for them to change the rules of interpretation.

However, if we're going to change those rules we better have clarity from the Lord that those rules need to be changed. But there's no evidence that God wants us to change the rules of interpretation.

For example, when we go to the first three chapters of Genesis, God is not pleased when we come up with progressive creationism, theistic evolution, or any kind of day-age theory. Instead, God is exalted as the Creator in the full glory of His creative power when we have a literal interpretation of the first three chapters of Genesis. Nothing in the text gives mandate to indicate that this descriptive account is something other than specific, literal, normal, and factual language. One cannot justify calling it poetry because a recent study conducted by one of our professors at The Master's College, using linguistic software to compare the difference between prose and poetry, led to the conclusion that the narrative account is distinctly prose and not poetry. We don't want anyone tampering with the beginning; why are we so tolerant of people tampering with the end?

We do not want to allow someone to arbitrarily introduce their own hermeneutic into Genesis, and yet we are content to allow people to introduce their own hermeneutics into prophetic passages throughout the Bible, and particularly in the book of Revelation. Where is the divine mandate on the pages of Scripture to do such a thing? What chapter and verse is that found in? Who then decides the new rules for engagement?

A Clarion Call for Change

Going back to my introductory thought, it is ironic that those who celebrate God's sovereign grace of unilateral, divine, unconditional, and irrevocable election to Christians unashamedly deny the same for elect Israel. This is a strange division, for Scripture teaches the perpetuity of the elect church to salvation glory, and in similar language Scripture affirms the perpetuity of ethnic Israel to a future salvation of a generation of Jews that will fulfill all the divine promises given to them by God. In both cases, this is the work of and the result of divine sovereign election.

Of all the people who could be premillennialist, it should be those who love sovereign election—Calvinists. Arminians make great amillennialists because the two views are consistent—God elects and preserves no one. We can leave amillennialism to the process theologians or the open theists, who think God is becoming progressively better because as every day goes by He gets more information to figure out whether or not in fact He can keep some of the promises He previously made. Let's leave amillennialism to the charismatics, the semi-pelagians, and other sorts who reject the security of salvation, since it makes sense with their theological position—Israel sinned, became apostate, killed the Son of God, and forfeited everything.

How is it possible to reconcile the idea that God is the only one who can determine who will be saved and yet proclaim that the church inherits all of Israel's promises because they do better than Israel? Amillennialism does not compute because it basically says Israel, based on their disobedience, forfeited all the promises. Do you think that they on their own could have done something to guarantee that they'd receive these pledges? If you think that Israel lost their place in God's economy because they did not do what they were supposed to, then you have rejected election and embraced Arminian theology. In Isaiah 45:4, God called Israel "my elect." He said, "For the sake of Jacob My servant, and Israel My chosen one, I have also called you by your name." Isaiah 65:9 speaks of Israel being God's elect and says that they will inherit the promise. In Isaiah 65:22, once again national Israel is called God's elect. God repeated this title a number of times in the Old Testament.

Now that leads us to the conclusion that if one's interpretation of God's election and Israel's promises is accurate, then their eschatology will be accurate as well. Never will you migrate from one view to another just depending on the last book you read, the last lecture you listened to, or the last influential person you interacted with.

How does one have a proper view of Israel? To get Israel right, you get the Old Testament covenants and promises right. To get the Old Testament covenants and promises right, you get the interpretation of Scripture right. To get the interpretation of Scripture right, you stay faithful to a legitimate hermeneutic. The end result of this is that God's integrity is upheld.

The Bible calls God "the God of Israel" more than 200 times. There are more than 2000 references to Israel in Scripture, with 73 New Testament uses of *Israel*. None of those references means anything but national Israel.

This includes Romans 9:6 and Galatians 6:16, which are the only two passages that amillennialists reference in their attempt to convince us that the two cancel out the other 1998. However, those two passages can easily be interpreted as a reference to Jews who were believers.

It should also be noted that Jews still exist today. That becomes an interesting fact when you ponder whether or not you've ever met a Hittite, an Amorite, or a Jebusite. Anybody know any of those folks? Do you know that the Israeli immigrant bureau in the land of Israel requires DNA tests where Jewish ancestry is questioned, and they actually know what Jewish DNA looks like? Somebody asked John Stott in a European conference what was the significance of Israel's existence today, and he replied, "It has no biblical significance." That's a strange answer, because three-fourths of Scripture is the story of Israel, and the nation is still in existence.

The foundation for an accurate understanding of eschatology is having a working concept of election and Israel. The two go together and are inseparable. How is it that we have come to understand election and totally missed Israel? I'm confident that God did not reveal prophetic truth in such a way to hide or obscure the truth, but to reveal it for our blessing, our motivation, and ultimately His glory. My words to you here are a call to reconnect these two truths. Return the sovereignty of God in election to its rightful place, and therefore return the nation Israel to its rightful place in God's redemptive history. As a result, all eschatology will unfold with magnificent beauty through the normal hermeneutic you can take to every passage.

Now that the Spirit of God is moving the church to reestablish the glorious high ground of sovereign grace in salvation, it is time to reestablish the equally high ground of sovereign grace for a future generation of ethnic Israel during the messianic earthly kingdom with the complete fulfillment of all God's promises to Israel.

A Tested Eschatology

I have thought through these great realities for almost 50 years. The clearer I understand sovereign electing grace, the clearer the place of Israel in God's redemptive plan gets. I have not moved away from the biblical eschatology I was convinced of when I began in the ministry. One of the benefits of being the pastor of Grace Community Church for nearly 40 years is that I'm forced to keep moving, since I can't preach old sermons. These dear people—can you imagine hearing the same preacher for almost 40 years? Not so good for them, but beneficial for me because I have had to continually teach all portions of the Bible. I'm getting close to preaching through the entirety of Luke, which leaves our church family with only the Gospel of Mark before I've preached through the entire New Testament. For 40 years I have taught and preached through every verse, every phrase, every word of the New Testament, then gone back and written commentaries. Through all of this my eschatology has had to stand the test of every New Testament verse. My conviction has not changed; it only has been strengthened and refined.

I've also preached through many Old Testament books. Early in my years here at Grace Community Church I started in Genesis. I've preached through prophetic books. In and out of Daniel, Ezekiel, Isaiah, Zechariah, and the minor prophets. A fair test of a cohesive eschatology is to drag it through every single text, and I've done my best to do exactly that. I am unwaveringly committed to the sovereign election of a future generation of Jews to salvation and the full inheritance of all the promises and covenants of God given to them in the Old Testament. This isn't a personal ambition; God's Word is at stake.

Dispensationalism?

Now, at this point I imagine some of you are saying, "Oh no—we came to a pastor's conference, and it's turned into a dispensational conference. Next thing he's going to do is drag out Clarence Larkin's charts, give out really nice leather-bound copies of the Scofield Study Bible, and then we'll all be gifted the Left Behind® series. He's probably going to tell us there are seven dispensations, two kingdoms, two new covenants, two ways of salvation." My response: Relax and forget dispensationalism, because I'm not talking about that. Even though, as a side note, every one of you is a dispensationalist. Let me test this hypothesis. Do you believe that God dealt with man one way before the Fall, after the Fall, before the law, after the law, before the cross, after the cross, now and in eternity? Exactly.

However, I reject the cartoon eschatology and the crazy interpretations

of the locusts of Revelation 9 being helicopters. I don't think that Henry
Kissinger is the Antichrist and that Hillary Clinton is the harlot of Babylon. Though I don't agree with all of dispensationalism, it is no more pecu-
liar than the interpretation of many amillennialists, who have fictionalized
that Jesus reads everything into AD 70. Another common objection is,
"Well, didn't the dispensationalists invent premillennialism?" In the modern era, two books reintroduced premillennial views, neither of them written by a dispensationalist. The first was called *The Pre-Millennial Advent
of Messiah*. It was written in 1836 by an Anglican named William Cuninghame.[4] The second was an English publication in 1827 written by Manuel Lacunza y Diaz, a Jesuit.[5] It is wrong to conclude that there is a direct
and necessary connection between all that is strange in dispensationalism
and a clear understanding of the kingdom.

The Whole Truth

When Frederick the Great asked his chaplain for proof of the truthfulness of the Bible, he said, "Give me a brief defense." His chaplain replied,
"I can do that in one word. Israel." Israel, understood as a people preserved
by God for an eschatological kingdom, has immense apologetic value. We
have to get the whole counsel of God right. We have to give the world the
truth about the end of history and the climactic glory of Christ and the
fulfillment of God's promises to Israel and the church. We delve into the
discussion with a series of questions.

Is the Old Testament Amillennial?

It is not legitimate to interpret the Old Testament as secondary to the
New Testament. If you say that, then the Old Testament cannot be rightly
interpreted apart from the New Testament, and you have denied the perspicuity of a large portion of God's Word. Walter Kaiser summarizes this
well when he writes that you end up having "a canon within a canon."
Without using the New Testament to reinterpret the Old, does the Old
Testament itself propound an amillennial view?

It's inappropriate to revoke the true meaning contained in the Old
Testament and make all of its promises related to the church. Even Paul
acknowledged that the church is a mystery not mentioned clearly in

previous revelation (Ephesians 3:1-6). The idea that the New Testament is the starting point for understanding the Old is where amillennialism comes from. Once again, if this is done, it damages the perspicuity or the clarity of the Old Testament in and of itself. It leads to exegetical spiritualization that goes beyond just prophetic texts and warrants the interpreter to lead New Testament Christian principles back into Old Testament texts, where they do not belong.

An example of this is what some individuals do with the book of Nehemiah. They interpret Nehemiah as being the Holy Spirit, the fallen walls of Jerusalem as the fallen walls of the human heart, and they say the Lord wants to rebuild the fallen heart by the use of mortar, which is speaking in tongues. Spiritualization puts the reader on a slippery slope.

It's rare to find a pastor who preaches the Old Testament with the interpretive lens of a person living at the time it was written. Please don't misunderstand what I mean—we can use the Old Testament for illustrations, we can use it for examples, and it has to have practical application to people in our cultural context. However, interpretation must begin with the clarity and perspicuity the original readers would have had.

Replacement theology ignores that principle and demands that the Old Testament promises be viewed through the lens of the New Testament. It also strikes a strange dichotomy since all the curses promised to Israel came to Israel and are still being poured out on them. If you're wondering whether the curses in the Old Testament were literal, you can see the tangible evidence of the nation of Israel bearing those curses. Yes, Israel is currently experiencing the promise of God that they will be perpetuated as an ethnic people; however, this current group of Jews that live in the world today, and in the nation Israel, are bearing a curse. They are apostate, they have rejected their Messiah, and they are under divine chastening. All the curses promised to Israel for disobedience to God came true and are coming true.

But now all of a sudden we're supposed to split all the passages of blessings and curses and say that Israel is experiencing literal curses, but the promises of blessing have been spiritualized and given to the church? Where is the textual justification for such a split interpretation? Wouldn't you think that whatever way the curses were fulfilled would set the standard for whatever way the blessings would be fulfilled? Also, wouldn't you expect that all of the prophecies that literally came to pass during Jesus' advent would set the pattern for how the prophecies connected to His second coming would come to pass?

Is the Old Testament amillennial? Of course not. If you affirm normal hermeneutics and the perspicuity of the Old Testament, then you cannot use the New Testament to reinterpret the Old. The totality of Scripture must be interpreted, preached, and taught as clear revelation from God that is to be understood, believed, and applied by the people to whom it was given.

What Are the Covenants?

To further understand this topic, we must ask a second question: What covenants are made in the Old Testament? The primary goal of this research is to behold the connection between these covenants and God's electing sovereignty. We read in Genesis 12:1, "Now the LORD said to Abram, 'Go forth from your country, and from your relatives and from your father's house.'" In this passage we have a great illustration of election. What did Abram do to set this in motion? Nothing, for Abram played no part in instituting this covenant. Now follow the use of the expression "I will": "And *I will* make you a great nation, and *I will* bless you, and make your name great; and so you shall be a blessing; and *I will* bless those who bless you, and the one who curses you *I will* curse. And in you all the families of the earth *will* be blessed" (verses 2-3). The expression is used five times. We see here sovereign, unilateral, and unconditional election.

In Genesis 15, Abram wanted confirmation of this covenant coming to fruition. "O Lord GOD, how may I know that I will possess it?" (Genesis 15:8). God's response: "'Bring me a three year old heifer, and a three year old female goat, and a three year old ram, and a turtledove, and a young pigeon.' Then he brought all these to Him and cut them in two, and laid each half opposite the other; but he did not cut the birds" (verses 9-10). Then the birds of prey came down upon the carcasses, but Abram drove them away.

Now what did God do here? He took these animals, cut them in half, set them opposite of each other, and there's a path going through these split animals and the two dead birds—one bird on each side. This relates to the term in Hebrew, "cut a covenant." When you cut a covenant or make a covenant, you put out blood sacrifices as a way of demonstrating the seriousness of the promise. God prepared what would be a very traditional and typical way to engage in making a covenant. Only this occasion is different because we read, "Now when the sun was going down, a deep sleep fell upon Abram; and behold, terror and great darkness fell upon him. God said to Abram, 'Know for certain that your descendants will be strangers in a land that is not theirs, where they will be enslaved and oppressed four hundred years'" (verses 12-13).

Well, does "four hundred years" actually mean four hundred? Yes it does! Our hermeneutic forces us to take that literally. And it's perfectly accurate because it's a prophecy of what will take place. "But I will also judge the nation whom they will serve, and afterward they will come out with many possessions. As for you, you shall go to your fathers in peace; you will be buried at a good old age" (verses 14-15).

Then we read in verse 17, "It came about when the sun had set, that it was very dark, and behold, there appeared a smoking oven and a flaming torch which passed between these pieces." God anesthetized Abram and God alone went through the pieces, visually indicating that this was a unilateral, unconditional, irrevocable promise that He made with Himself. There were no conditions for Abraham to fulfill. For on that day, the Lord made a covenant with Abraham, and it is a covenant that does not end.

We jump to Genesis 17:7: "I will establish my covenant between Me and you and your descendants after you throughout their generations for an everlasting covenant, to be God to you and to your descendants after you." God elected Abraham, elected the nation that would come out of his loins, and made a covenant and a promise to be their God. This is the foundational covenant in the Bible, a unilateral and unconditional promise of the Lord.

The Mosaic Covenant

Fast-forward to when God gave the Mosaic Covenant to Israel—it became very apparent how sinful they were. Yet even in the midst of Israel's blatant sin, apostasy, idolatry, and violation of God's law, the nation still continued to be the object of His covenant love. In Ezekiel 16 there is a staggering chronicle by God of His choice of Israel. He speaks of Israel in graphic terms, comparing their election to finding a baby thrown away in a field. "On the day you were born your navel cord was not cut, nor were you washed with water for cleansing; you were not rubbed with salt [which they did to disinfect children] or even wrapped in cloths. No eye looked with pity on you to do any of these things for you, to have compassion on you. Rather you were thrown out into the open field, for you were abhorred on the day you were born" (Ezekiel 16:4-5). God said, "When I passed by you and saw you squirming in your blood, I said to you while you were in your blood, 'Live!' Yes, I said to you while you were in your blood, 'Live!'" (verse 6). There again we see God's sovereign election.

The story goes on to show how God took Israel as an unfaithful wife, cleansed her, and made her His own. "Moreover, you played the harlot with the Assyrians because you were not satisfied; you played the harlot with them and still were not satisfied" (verse 28). Then in verse 36 we read, "Your lewdness was poured out and your nakedness uncovered through your harlotries with your lovers and with all your detestable idols, and because of the blood of your sons which you gave to idols." Indictment after indictment, we see that God is furious with them. Nevertheless, we read,

> "I will remember My covenant with you in the days of your
> youth, and I will establish an everlasting covenant with you.
> Then you will remember your ways and be ashamed when you
> receive your sisters, *both* your older and your younger; and I
> will give them to you as daughters, but not because of your covenant. Thus I will establish My covenant with you, and you
> shall know that I am the LORD, so that you may remember
> and be ashamed and never open your mouth anymore because
> of your humiliation, when I have forgiven you for all that you
> have done," the Lord GOD declares (verses 60-63).

This is a reiteration of the terms of the covenant in the face of Israel's history of defection, disobedience, and apostasy. God's decision to set His love on Israel was in no way determined by Israel's performance nor by

Israel's national worthiness, but purely on the basis of His independent, uninfluenced, sovereign grace (Deuteronomy 7:7-8). The Lord alone is the sole party responsible to fulfill the obligations, and there are no conditions which Abram or any other Jew could fulfill on their own.

A parallel can be made with the Christian's experience. Believers do not come to Christ on their own, but are given life by the Spirit of God according to His will. And the Lord alone is the sole party responsible to fulfill the obligations. Obedience is not the condition that determines fulfillment. Rather, divine sovereign power is the condition that determines obedience, which leads to fulfillment. Therefore, when God gave the unilateral covenant, He knew He would have to produce the obedience in the future to fulfill this plan.

The Davidic Covenant

After the Mosaic Covenant, God gave the Davidic Covenant, which was instituted in 2 Samuel 7. It is here that God promised to David that he would have a greater son who will have an everlasting kingdom. This covenant is an expansion of the Abrahamic Covenant: "I will raise up your descendant after you, who will come forth from you, and I will establish his kingdom. He shall build a house for My name, and I will establish the throne of his kingdom forever" (2 Samuel 7:12-13). God promised to Abraham a seed, a land, and a nation; of course that embodies the kingdom and the promise of a perfect king. In establishing the Davidic Covenant, once again we see God use the phrase "I will." God is the one who accomplishes His work.

It is important to clarify that this is not to say that the Abrahamic Covenant is only for Israel. We all participate in its spiritual blessings. When it comes to the Abrahamic and Davidic Covenants, all believers will participate, even those not of Israel, because we experience salvation and are citizens of the kingdom.

The New Covenant

The final covenant is the New Covenant. There can be no fulfillment of the promises God gave to Abraham or David apart from salvation. And throughout history there has always been a faithful remnant of

Israel—those who did not bow the knee to Ba'al. God has always had a people, His chosen. And not all Israel is the true Israel of God. Isaiah 6:13 reminds us that God will have a holy remnant, but in the future there will be a salvation of ethnic Israel on a national level. That is precisely the message of Jeremiah 31—the New Covenant given to Israel.

We enjoy discussing this covenant because we participate in the salvific provision of the New Covenant ratified in the death and resurrection of Christ. However, it is essential to remember that the application of the New Covenant is in a special way given to a future generation of Jews. "'Behold, days are coming,' declares the LORD, 'when I will make a new covenant with the house of Israel and with the house of Judah, not like the covenant which I made with their fathers in the day I took them by the hand to bring them out of the land of Egypt, My covenant which they broke, although I was a husband to them'" (Jeremiah 31:31-32). The Mosaic Covenant was not a covenant that could save, but this New Covenant from the Lord will change everything. What warrant do amillennialists have to say that the direct reference to "Israel" does not mean national Israel?

"I will put my law within them and on their heart I will write it; and I will be their God, and they shall be My people" (verse 33). "I will forgive their iniquity, and their sin I will remember no more" (verse 34). Is it possible that God has changed His mind about doing this for His people? "Thus says the LORD, who gives the sun for light by day and the fixed order of the moon and the stars for light by night, who stirs up the sea so that its waves roar; the LORD of hosts is His name: 'If this fixed order departs from before Me,' declares the LORD, 'then the offspring of Israel also will cease from being a nation before Me forever'" (verses 35-36). I haven't noticed that happen yet. Have you? There isn't another way to understand this passage other than the clear and literal meaning. If this text does not mean what it just said, then it's incomprehensible.

The New Covenant promises the salvation that incorporates all the promises of the Abrahamic Covenant, the Davidic Covenant, and all the extended promises throughout the entire Old Testament. What is the key feature? God will put His law within them; on their heart He will write it. He will be their God, and He will forgive their iniquity.

The parallel passage of this promise is found in Ezekiel 36:24-27:

I will take you from the nations, gather you from all the lands and bring you into your own land. Then I will sprinkle clean water on you, and you will be clean; I will cleanse you from all your filthiness and from all your idols. Moreover, I will give you a new heart and put a new spirit within you; and I will remove the heart of stone from your flesh and give you a heart of flesh. I will put My Spirit within you and cause you to walk in My statutes, and you will be careful to observe My ordinances.

The only way an individual is capable of walking in God's statutes and obeying His ordinances is if God Himself causes them to do it. When God gave unilateral, unconditional, sovereign, and gracious promises to an elect people, He guaranteed He would fulfill those promises through His divine power. When God said such covenant promises are irrevocable, we cannot, without impunity and guilt, for any seemingly convenient idea or assumption, say they are void.

Well, what about Israel's apostasy? Doesn't that revoke the promises? Understand that the New Covenant promises given in Jeremiah and Ezekiel were given to Israel at the time when the nation was under divine judgment for apostasy. These blessings were not given when all was well and the people were living in obedience to God. At the time of this prophecy Israel is apostate, living out of the land, and God still says that even this rebellion will not revoke His promises.

Another fair question that arises is, "Didn't Israel reject their Messiah?" One of the strange theories of dispensationalism is that Jesus came and offered the kingdom, and because unbelieving Jews did not accept it and killed Him, He came up with Plan B, which entailed giving the kingdom to the church. That is completely wrong because the cross was not Plan B. We can read the description of what would happen at the cross in Psalm 22. Isaiah 53 prophetically described the crucifixion and the Suffering Servant, Jesus. The cross has always been part of the plan.

But how does national Israel connect with the cross? In Zechariah 12:10, we read, "They will look on Me whom they have pierced; and they will mourn for Him, as one mourns for an only son, and they will weep bitterly over Him like the bitter weeping over a firstborn." Then in Zechariah 13:1:

"In that day a fountain will be opened for the house of David and for the inhabitants of Jerusalem, for sin and for impurity." A day will come when Israel will be saved and the totality of the New Covenant will be fulfilled! And if you continue reading into Zechariah 14, you'll learn about the coming of the kingdom. Zechariah chapters 12 to 14 do not make sense apart from a premillennial view.

Were the Israelites in Jesus' Day Amillennial?

In an effort to answer this third question, Emil Schurer wrote a helpful study of first-century Jewish eschatology. It was first published in 1880, and a more recent edition was released by Hendrickson Publishers.[6] Shurer stated that the ancient Israelites believed the Messiah's coming would be preceded by a time of trouble. They believed that before the Messiah arrived, Elijah would come as a forerunner. They also believed that the Messiah would be the personal son of David, that He would have special powers to set up His kingdom, and that all the Abrahamic and Davidic Covenant promises would be fulfilled in Him.

They also believed that Israel would repent and be saved at the coming of the Anointed One, the kingdom would be established in Israel with Jerusalem at the center, and the messianic influence would extend across the world. As a result, the world would be renovated, peace and righteousness would dominate, and all people would worship the Messiah. This worship would involve a reinstituted temple. The culmination of this kingdom would be final judgment, and after that, the eternal state. That's Jewish pre-New Testament eschatology. And it lines up perfectly with the premillennialist view.

Schurer is not the only evidence for this. Zacharias, the priestly father of John the Baptist, believed this. In the latter part of Luke 1, Zacharias's proclamation stems from the Old Testament passages about the Abrahamic, Davidic, and New Covenants. Zacharias knew what was happening—that the coming Messiah meant the covenants were to be fulfilled.

Was Jesus Amillennial?

This fourth question is one of the most important we must answer. We read what Luke wrote about the resurrected Christ:

The first account I composed, Theophilus, about all that Jesus began to do and teach, until the day when He was taken up to heaven, after He had by the Holy Spirit given orders to the apostles whom He had chosen. To these He also presented Himself alive after His suffering, by many convincing proofs, appearing to them over a period of forty days and speaking of the things concerning the kingdom of God (Acts 1:1-3).

Jesus spent His final 40 days with the disciples talking about the things concerning the kingdom of God. If Jesus was amillennial, this was His moment to launch amillennialism. But we see that after 40 days of instruction about the kingdom, the disciples were still confident that the kingdom, for national Israel, was still a future event. They did not ask if the kingdom would come to Israel. Instead, they asked when: "Lord, is it at this time You are restoring the kingdom to Israel?" (verse 6).

How did Jesus respond? Did He say, "Where did you get such a foolish idea? Where did you come up with that concept? Haven't you been listening to Me during the last forty days? I'm an amillennialist. How bizarre to think that I'm going to restore the kingdom to Israel. You didn't hear me—the church is the new Israel."

But Jesus didn't say there isn't going to be a kingdom. Rather, He responded, "It is not for you to know times or epochs which the Father has fixed by His own authority" (verse 7).

In Acts 1:7, the Greek verb "fixed" is in the middle voice, so it's better translated "the Father has fixed for Himself." It's about the Father's glory, exaltation, and the world finally experiencing paradise regained. The ultimate goal here is singular and unilateral. There is no Replacement Theology in the theology of Jesus; there is no supersessionism. This movement to establish that there is no earthly kingdom for Israel is absolutely foreign to the Old Testament, foreign to the New Testament, and foreign to Jesus.

Were the Apostles Amillennial?

If the Israelites in Jesus' day and Jesus Himself did not hold to the amillennial view, then what about Peter? Was he the first amillennialist? To answer this fifth question, we listen in on Peter's sermon:

The God of Abraham, Isaac and Jacob, the God of our fathers,
has glorified His servant Jesus, the one whom you delivered
and disowned in the presence of Pilate, when he had decided to
release Him. But you disowned the Holy and Righteous One
and asked for a murderer to be granted to you, but put to death
the Prince of life, the one whom God raised from the dead, a
fact to which we are witnesses (Acts 3:13-15).

"But the things which God announced beforehand by the mouth of all
the prophets, that His Christ would suffer, He has thus fulfilled" (verse
18). This is a statement that we take literally; therefore, the next phrase
that comes out of Peter's mouth should be taken literally as well: "Therefore repent and return, so that your sins may be wiped away, in order that
times of refreshing may come from the presence of the Lord" (verse 19).
"Times of refreshing" refers to the future kingdom. "That He may send
Jesus, the Christ appointed for you, whom heaven must receive until the
period of restoration of all things about which God spoke by the mouth
of His holy prophets from ancient time" (verses 20-21). I especially love
verse 25: "It is you who are the sons of the prophets and of the covenant
which God made with your fathers."

Peter did not cancel the covenant; he reinforced the validity of it: "Saying to Abraham, 'And in your seed all the families of the earth shall be
blessed.' For you first, God raised up His Servant and sent Him to bless
you by turning every one of you from your wicked ways" (verses 25-26).
Peter had the perfect opportunity to nullify these promises, and yet he
reminded his Jewish listeners that they were the sons of the covenant.

Was James an amillennialist? Read what he said:

Simeon has related how God first concerned Himself about
taking from among the Gentiles a people for His name. With
this the words of the Prophets agree, just as it is written, "After
these things I will return, and I will rebuild the tabernacle of
David which has fallen, and I will rebuild its ruins, and I will
restore it, so that the rest of mankind may seek the Lord, and
all the Gentiles who are called by My name," says the Lord,
who makes these things known from long ago (Acts 15:14-18).

The acceptance of the Gentiles was not the cancellation of Israel's promises. Instead, after Gentile conversion, God will rebuild the tabernacle of David, which has fallen, entailing that the Davidic Covenant and messianic promises will be fulfilled.

Maybe the apostle Paul was the first amillennial? He wrote in Romans 3:1-4, "What advantage has the Jew? Or what is the benefit of circumcision? Great in every respect. First of all, that they were entrusted with the oracles of God. What then? If some did not believe, their unbelief will not nullify the faithfulness of God, will it? May it never be!" If Paul had held the amillennialist position, he would have written, "Absolutely, it nullifies the promise of God." But he didn't do that. Note what he said:

> It is not as though the word of God has failed. For they are not all Israel who are descended from Israel [that is to say they are not all true Israel]; nor are they all children because they are Abraham's descendants, but: "through Isaac your descendants will be named." That is, it is not the children of the flesh who are children of God, but the children of the promise are regarded as descendants (Romans 9:6-8).

Just because some Jews hadn't come to belief didn't mean that God's faithfulness had been nullified. And just because there are some whom God chooses doesn't mean that He is not going to choose a whole duly-constituted generation of Jews to fulfill His promises.

Then perhaps most notably we see what Romans 11:26 says: "So all Israel will be saved." How else can you interpret that? One way is to say that Paul was not referring to national Israel. But where in the text does it say it's not Israel? "Just as it is written, 'The deliverer will come from Zion, He will remove ungodliness from Jacob.' 'This is My covenant with them, when I take away their sins'" (verse 26). The Israelites are enemies at the present time, but that is for the sake of the Gentiles. Why can we be sure that eventually God will save them? "For the gifts and the calling of God are irrevocable" (verse 29). If it depended on the people of Israel to obey God on their own, then theirs was an impossible task from the start. Only the One who made the promise can enable the obedience that is connected to the fulfillment of the promise.

The Danger of Replacement Theology

Ronald Diprose wrote an excellent work titled *Israel and the Church*.[7] It first appeared as a PhD dissertation in Italian and has no connection to traditional dispensationalism. It shows how the effect of Replacement Theology helped to form the church of the Dark Ages—he explains how the church went from the New Testament concept to the sacramental institutional system of the Dark Ages, which we know as Roman Catholicism.

Diprose lays much of the blame at the feet of Replacement Theology, which stems from Augustine, Origen, and Justin. Why did the church implement altars, sacrifices, a sign parallel to circumcision, a priesthood, ceremonial rituals, and reintroduce mystery by speaking in a language that most people could not understand? Diprose traced the Roman Catholic ecclesiology to the influence of causing the church to be the new Israel. Replacement Theology justifies bringing in all the trappings of Judaism.

Another negative effect of Replacement Theology is the damage it does to evangelistic outreach to Jewish people. Imagine that you're speaking to a Jewish person and you say, "Jesus is the Messiah."

The response: "Really? Where is His established kingdom?"

"It's already here," you say.

The Jewish person's retort: "If that's the case, then why are we still being killed and persecuted? Why don't we have the land that was promised to us? Why isn't the Messiah reigning in Jerusalem, and why aren't peace and joy and gladness dominating the world? Why isn't the desert blooming?"

Then you say, "Oh no, you don't understand. All that's not going to take place literally. You're actually not God's people anymore; we are."

Then the Jewish person will respond with this devastating comment: "If this is the kingdom of Jesus, then Jesus is not the Messiah the Tanakh promises."

However, if you tell that nonbelieving Jew that God will keep every single promise He made to Israel, and that God is preparing for a great day of restoration for the Jewish people, then you have a chance to communicate to that individual. But you have to look to Psalm 22, Isaiah 53, and Zechariah 12:10 to understand that first the Messiah had to come, die, and be raised on the third day to ratify the New Covenant so He could forgive people's sins and inaugurate the kingdom.

A Final Plea

As pastors, we have to get divine, sovereign, gracious, unconditional, unilateral, irrevocable election right, and we have to get God, Israel, and eschatology right. When we do, then we can open our Bibles and preach our heart out of any text and say what it says without having to scramble around and find some bizarre interpretation that fits a specific theological system.

Get it right, and God is glorified. Get it right, and Christ is exalted. Get it right, and the Holy Spirit is honored. Get it right, and Scripture is clear. Get it right, and the greatest historical illustration of God's work in the world is visible. Get it right, and the meaning of mystery in the New Testament is maintained. Get it right, and the straightforward meaning of the text is intact and Scripture wasn't written for mystics. Get it right, and the chronology of prophetic literature is intact. Get it right, and your historical worldview is complete. Get it right, and the practical benefit of eschatology is released on your people. Get it right!

A literal millennial kingdom of the eschaton is the only view that honors sovereign electing grace, honors the truthfulness of God's promises, honors the teachings of Old Testament prophets, the teachings of Jesus, and the teachings of the New Testament writers. Make your church a second-coming church, and make your life a second-coming life.

PRAYER

Father, what a glorious, transcendent theme. May we live in the light of the coming of Christ. May we know that Your Word can be trusted and that we can preach every verse and proclaim what it clearly states. Thank You for these precious men who are here at the conference. Lord, fill us all with joy in the truth and in the privilege of serving You. In Christ's name. Amen.

HEAVEN ON EARTH: EXPLORING THE GLORIES OF THE ETERNAL STATE

"According to His promise we are looking
for new heavens and a new earth,
in which righteousness dwells."

2 PETER 3:13

11

Heaven on Earth: Exploring the Glories of the Eternal State

Michael Vlach

Shepherds' Conference 2013

Selected Scriptures

M any discussions on eschatology focus on the rapture, Tribulation, and millennium. Consequently, the eternal state often gets left out of detailed consideration. Yet the eternal state ought to excite us. When we look at the fallen world and experience its effects, it is good to think about our ultimate destiny. The new heavens and new earth with its New Jerusalem is where we will spend eternity. Even the thousand-year millennial kingdom, as long as it is, is significantly less than eternity.

Second Peter 3:13 reads, "According to His promise we are looking for new heavens and a new earth, in which righteousness dwells." The new heavens and new earth are our ultimate destiny, and it is to them that we should be looking. Even the intermediate heaven, where saints go when they die, is temporary. It will give way to the new earth and the New Jerusalem. Therefore, we cannot neglect this important doctrine.

Mistakes to Avoid

There are two mistakes to avoid when studying the eternal state. The first is avoiding this topic. For most of church history this has been a problem. Compared to other doctrines, there are not many works treating the eternal state.[1] A second mistake involves looking at eternity through what can be called "spiritual vision model" glasses. This occurs when we overspiritualize the eternal state and treat it as so transcendent and "other-than" that we lose how real it is. The spiritual vision model is a paradigm or approach to God's purposes that elevates spiritual realities to the exclusion of physical realities.

Spiritual vision thinking can be traced to the philosopher Plato, who made a strong distinction in value between spiritual and physical matters. His ideas influenced both Jewish and Christian scholars at times. Unfortunately, when Christians think about their eternal home they often perceive it as a static, colorless, spiritual existence. Studies have shown that roughly two-thirds of Americans think heaven is a bodiless spiritual existence. But that is not what the Bible teaches. When God created the world, He declared it "very good." This included the physical realm. Because the creation has a physical dimension, so too will the new earth.

We should not overspiritualize our future home and think God's purposes are only spiritual and not material. You may be familiar with cartoons where people in heaven are seen on a cloud with wings and a halo. That is a common cultural conception—heaven is static, still, contemplative, and boring. Many people think of heaven in those terms. There are even Christians who wonder, "Is heaven boring?" Nothing could be further from the truth.

Christian leaders need to teach people about our eternal home on the new earth. Doing so helps give people hope! If we are making the eternal state into something that it's not, then our hope is perverted. We must seriously examine passages related to the eternal state and draw sound conclusions when possible.

Revelation 21–22 is the most specific passage about the eternal state. There are some things in these chapters that we can know with a high degree of confidence. Also, some matters are more difficult to understand. Sometimes people can err on one of two sides. One is to think they can be certain on the meaning of every detail. Another is avoiding these chapters altogether.

I have put together a list of ten study points on the eternal state to help us better understand the glories of our home to come. But first, let's look at three key presuppositions:

Key Presuppositions

First, we can have real and sufficient knowledge about the eternal state. This does not mean perfect or exhaustive knowledge. But just because we do not have exhaustive knowledge does not mean we cannot have true knowledge. God has revealed truths about our eternal destiny, and He wants us to understand them.

Second, the eternal state is not just a colorful way of describing our present salvation experience. It is not simply a picturesque description of our salvation. Second Corinthians 5:17 and Galatians 6:15 indicate we are new creatures in Christ, but Revelation 21–22 is describing the ultimate destiny of God's people. The details in Revelation 21–22 explain a real, literal, and tangible place that the people of God will dwell in.

Third, the eternal state of Revelation 21–22 follows the millennial kingdom described in Revelation 20:1-6. The chronology in Revelation describes a coming period of tribulation (chapters 6–18). This period culminates in the return of Jesus Christ to earth (chapter 19). Following Jesus' return to earth is the thousand-year reign of Jesus and His saints on the earth (chapter 20). Then the glories of the eternal state will occur (chapters 21–22:5).

Ten Considerations About the Eternal State

The Beginning and the End

First, strong parallels exist between the creation account in Genesis 1–2 and the new creation described in Revelation 21–22. The new creation is a restoration of the original and very good creation of God. So it is helpful to go back to the very beginning and then look at the very end. To use theological terminology, we should study both protology (beginning things) and eschatology (last things). We should study Genesis 1–2 and Revelation 21–22. As we do, issues regarding the fall and the work of Christ at His first coming become clearer.

There are striking comparisons between the first two chapters of the Bible and the last two chapters. In both, we see God as creator and maker.

Genesis 1 says God created the heavens and the earth. Then in Revelation 21:1, John sees "a new heaven and a new earth." In the Genesis account, God said, "'Let there be light'; and there was light" (verse 3). Then in Revelation, there is no need for a lamp or light because the glory of God will illumine His people (22:5).

In Genesis 1–2 we learn about the Garden of Eden. In Revelation 21–22 we see the new heavens and earth and the New Jerusalem. Concerning the presence of God with man, the Lord God walked in the garden in the cool of the day with Adam. Then we are told in Revelation 21:3, "Behold, the tabernacle of God is among men, and He will dwell among them."

In Genesis, death was promised for disobedience—"In the day that you eat from it you will surely die" (Genesis 2:17). But Revelation 21:4 tells us death is removed. When it comes to the curse, Genesis 3:17 states, "Cursed is the ground because of you." But Revelation 22:3 tells us, "There will no longer be any curse." In the Genesis account, there was a river that flowed out of Eden. And there is a river in Revelation 22:1—the river of the water of life. Also, the tree of life is prominent in Genesis 2–3. After that we no longer see the tree of life. But Revelation 22:2 states: "On either side of the river was the tree of life." The tree of life was in the Garden of Eden, and it will show up again in the New Jerusalem.

With Genesis 1:26-28 we discover God's mandate for mankind to rule and subdue the earth as God's mediator. Then the last verse about the New Jerusalem in Revelation 22:5 says God's people will reign on the earth—"They will reign forever and ever."

Satan deceived God's image bearers in Genesis 3, but when you get to Revelation 20:1-3, Satan is incarcerated in a spiritual prison called the abyss. A thousand years later he is sentenced to the lake of fire forever. The tempter is removed.

The importance of nations is discussed in Genesis 10–11, where we find an extensive table of nations listing people groups from the sons of Noah. Then in Revelation 21:24 we read, "The nations will walk by [the New Jerusalem's] light, and the kings of the earth will bring their glory into it." From Genesis 10 onward, nations are in conflict, but in Revelation 21–22 nations are at peace. Revelation 22:2 states that "the leaves of the tree [of life] were for the healing of the nations."

Do you see a pattern? As we study Genesis 1–2 and then Revelation 21–22, we see a strong connection between the creation account and the new creation account.

When it comes to the issue of the eternal state in the Old Testament, the prophets did not always make clear distinctions between the coming intermediate kingdom (i.e., the millennium) and the eternal state. When prophets like Isaiah looked at the days of Messiah and things to come, they offered details that could be true of both the millennial and eternal kingdom. However, later on in the scheme of progressive revelation, it becomes clearer that there is a distinction between the millennial kingdom and the eternal kingdom.

In Isaiah 65:20, we read that in a coming period, "the youth will die at the age of one hundred and the one who does not reach the age of one hundred will be thought accursed." The prophet is telling us that if someone were to die at the age of 100, we would think, *What happened? What went wrong?*

Can we say that is true in this present age we live in? If somebody dies at the age of 100, do we say, "Wow, that person must have done something wrong. What happened?" No; in fact, we are impressed that the person lived for so long. On the other hand, we know death won't occur in the eternal state. Death will have been removed. That tells us Isaiah 65:20 must refer to a different period. In what era is dying at age 100 viewed as a premature death? Certainly not in this age, since most people die before age 85. And it certainly cannot be in the eternal state, since no one will die at that time. The only era in which death at age 100 could be considered premature, then, is the intermediate kingdom known as the millennium (Revelation 20:1-6).

First Corinthians 15:20-28 explains that Jesus will bring the original creation back into conformity to the Father's will. Once Jesus successfully completes His reign upon the earth and has subjected all things to Himself, He will hand the kingdom over to God the Father and subject Himself to the Father. After the Messiah has reigned over every square inch of

this previously rebellious planet, a transition will occur to the eternal kingdom, when God will be all in all (1 Corinthians 15:24, 28).

Revelation 21:1–22:5 describes the new earth and the New Jerusalem.
Alan Johnson wrote: "It is remarkable that John's picture of the final age
to come focuses not on a platonic ideal heaven or distant paradise but on
the reality of a new earth and heaven. God originally created the earth and
heaven to be man's permanent home."[2]

People often think of eternity as a purely spiritual destiny. Many are
under the impression that our ultimate destiny is escaping earth and anything physical. Supposedly we will live in a spiritual realm forever. But that
is not the picture that Scripture paints.

Replacement or Renewal?

The second detail is that Revelation 21:1 says the new heaven and new
earth will replace the present heaven and earth. The present heaven and
earth will pass away. But what does this mean? Here we run into an issue
on which many godly and intelligent Bible teachers disagree. The disagreement is not whether there is going to be a real, tangible, physical new earth.
But there is debate concerning the relationship of the present earth with
the coming new earth. Two differing views are: (1) an annihilation of the
present earth with a replacement new earth, or (2) a renewal of the present earth so the new earth is this present earth restored. Some believe the
present earth is annihilated and replaced by an entirely new earth. Others
believe the new earth is this present planet purged and restored.

Both sides point to evidence for their views. In favor of the annihilation view is Revelation 20:11, which speaks about the earth and heaven
fleeing away. Second Peter 3:10-12 talks about destruction by fire and the
elements being burned up. Some say this indicates a removal of the present order of things so much that there needs to be an entirely new universe. Psalm 102:26 states, "Even they [earth and heavens] will perish…
all of them will wear out like a garment." Jesus said, "Heaven and earth
will pass away" (Matthew 24:35). These texts are viewed as evidence that
there will be an entirely new, out-of-nothing creation that replaces the
current earth.

On the other hand, the renewal view makes much of Romans 8, which indicates the creation will be glorified when man is glorified. To explain further, when man fell, the creation was subjected to futility. The ground was cursed. But we are told, in verse 20, that it was subjected "in hope." Creation is personified as longing to be set free from its current corruption and slavery. When man is glorified, the earth is glorified as well.

Key biblical terms point to a renewal of the earth. Jesus speaks of a coming "regeneration" of the cosmos in Matthew 19:28. Regeneration can mean "renewal" in the sense of remaking something that was marred. In Colossians 1:20, Paul says Jesus will "reconcile all things to Himself, having made peace through the blood of His cross." The "all things" in this context of Colossians 1:15-20 involves everything that has been created, including the world.

In Acts 3:21, Peter predicts a coming "restoration of all things" that the Old Testament prophets wrote about. This language of regeneration, reconciliation, and restoration refers to fixing what previously was broken. They do not seem consistent with an annihilation view.

Those who hold to a renewal view sometimes argue that this view highlights God's victory in saving the creation He created and deemed "very good" (Genesis 1:31). Satan does not get the victory over God's "very good" creation—God does! So God does not send His original creation into oblivion; He restores it!

I believe the restoration view is correct. The evidence, particularly Romans 8, indicates a strong parallel between creation and man. When man fell, creation fell. When man is glorified, creation will be glorified. When it comes to our future, God does not annihilate and start over with an entirely new person. We will receive a resurrection body, but there is continuity with who we are now. The fiery destruction of the universe in 2 Peter 3 is best understood in the sense of purging and purifying, not annihilation. The destruction of the earth in 2 Peter 3 is likened to the destruction of the world by the flood in Noah's day. This was a global catastrophic destruction, but it was not an annihilation of earth.

Continuity or Discontinuity?

Third, Second Corinthians 5:17 says, "If anyone is in Christ, he is a new creature; the old things passed away; behold, new things have come."

When a person becomes a Christian, he becomes a new creature. Old things have passed away. But a Christian does not become an entirely different person. There is still a one-to-one correspondence between who we are now and who we will be in the future. That is true of Jesus, who was the "first fruits" of the resurrection (1 Corinthians 15:20). When Jesus came out of the grave, He was transformed and glorified, but He was still the same person.

Revelation 21:1 says, "Then I saw a new heaven and new earth; for the first heaven and the first earth passed away." So clearly there is a discontinuity between the present universe and the one to come. The question is, are we looking at a discontinuity in the sense of a total replacement? This passage could be emphasizing removal of the world tainted by sin to one purged from the effects of sin.

Revelation 21:1 also tells us that no sea was seen on the new earth. There have been different understandings of what it means that there will be no sea. Some believe that "sea" in Revelation represents chaos. Daniel talks about bad Gentile powers coming from the sea, and in the ancient world, the sea was viewed as being hostile. While John wrote the book of Revelation, he was surrounded by the sea as he was imprisoned. However, if we are talking about a literal new heaven, a literal new earth, and a literal New Jerusalem, then it seems a bit odd to conclude that "sea" is just figurative for chaos.

Others believe that the statement "there is no longer any sea" simply means there will be no bodies of water or aquatic life on the new earth. Still others say that the saltwater seas and oceans that separate men now in a fallen world will be removed, but this does not mean the total removal of all bodies of water, such as large lakes, rivers, etc. For example, a river is mentioned in Revelation chapter 22. Perhaps this river flows to other bodies of water.

The New Jerusalem

A fourth detail of the eternal state is the holy city, the New Jerusalem. This New Jerusalem was the ultimate hope of Abraham, as stated in the book of Hebrews. When it comes to this city, there have been some different views on what it actually is. Some have argued that the New

Jerusalem itself is the new earth. So nothing exists outside the New Jerusalem because the New Jerusalem is new earth.

The next view is that the New Jerusalem will reside upon the new earth. This view is more likely. John saw the new heaven and earth, and then he spoke of a New Jerusalem coming down from heaven. This seems to be the capital city of the new earth. Revelation 21:24-26 mentions "the nations… and the kings of the earth [who] will bring their glory into [the city]." That the nations will bring their glory *into* the city shows activity *outside* of the New Jerusalem. These nations outside the city will bring their cultural contributions into the city.

God's Presence

Fifth, God will establish His presence fully with men. Revelation 21:3 says, "I heard a loud voice from the throne saying, 'Behold, the tabernacle of God is among men, and He will dwell among them, and they shall be His people, and God Himself will be among them.'" In the Old Testament, God's presence resided in the tabernacle and then the temple. With Jesus' coming, God resided with men. In this age between the two comings of Jesus, the Holy Spirit resides in His people. In the coming millennial kingdom, Jesus will be physically present on earth while the Holy Spirit continues to reside among God's people. Yet in the eternal state, the full presence of God will be on the new earth. The Father, the Lamb, and of course the Holy Spirit will dwell on the new earth with humankind.

In Revelation 21:3, some translations read, "They shall be His people." The literal translation is "peoples" (Greek, *laoi*) and probably refers to "the nations" of 21:24-26.

The Death of Death

Sixth, God will remove the negative aspects of the previous world. Revelation 21:4 declares: "He will wipe away every tear from their eyes; and there will no longer be any death; there will no longer be any mourning, or crying, or pain; the first things have passed away." The day is coming when all the negative effects of the fall will be removed. There will be no more death, no more mourning, no more crying, and no more pain.

Living in a fallen world makes it seem like the negative aspects of sin are going to continue forever, but they are not! Sin and its effects will be removed.

The Wicked Will Not Enter

The seventh detail about the eternal state is that believers will inherit the new earth while unbelievers will be barred from it. Revelation 21:8 states, "The cowardly and unbelieving and abominable and murderers and immoral persons and sorcerers and idolaters and all liars, their part will be in the lake that burns with fire and brimstone, which is the second death." We are reminded that the story does not end well for everyone. God's people will inherit the new earth, but the wicked will be banished from it. As preachers and teachers, we must be careful that we do not present the new earth and heaven as everyone's destiny, because it is not. Salvation comes through faith in Christ alone. Without this, no one will participate in the new earth.

Exploring the New Jerusalem

Eighth, from Revelation 21:10 onward we read a glorious description of the New Jerusalem. According to Revelation 21:12, the city will have "a great and high wall, with twelve gates." At the gates will be 12 angels, and the names of the 12 tribes of Israel will be written on the gates. In verse 13, we read, "There were three gates on the east and three gates on the north and three gates on the south and three gates on the west." This suggests continuity with the old earth because navigational directions still exist. Verse 14 reveals that the city wall will have 12 foundation stones with the names of the 12 apostles on them. Verse 15 says the city and the wall can be measured: "The one who spoke with me had a gold measuring rod to measure the city, and its gates and its wall."

We are then given the dimensions of this great city: "The city is laid out as a square," which means the length, width, and height will be equal. "Its length is as great as the width; and he measured the city with the rod, fifteen hundred miles; its length and width and height are equal" (verse 16).

There are four different understandings as to what 1500 miles in width, length, and height actually means. Some say this refers to a pyramid shape. A more popular view is that the city is in the shape of a cube, and that we can draw connections with the shape of past temples and the Holy of Holies. The most holy place in the temple was in the shape of a cube, so this would mean that the New Jerusalem would be like an encased temple or building.

Still others have argued that the shape is that of a square and not a cube, so John was referring to a large land mass surrounded by a wall. Another view is that architectural shape is not in view here, but rather, emphasis is being placed on the city's perfection.

Another question with regard to the city is its sheer magnitude. The predominant view is that the city is 1500 miles long, wide, and high. If that is the case, the area covered would be 2,250,000 square miles, which is extremely large. The length and width of the city is roughly half the size of the United States.

A lesser-held view is that the city is 1500 miles in totality, which entails that its length, width, and height add up to 1500 miles. So if it is in the shape of a square, then each of the sides measures 375 miles. If you accept those estimates, then the city would be more the size of a large Midwestern state in the United States.

We learn about the size of the wall in verse 17: "He measured its wall, seventy-two yards, according to human measurements, which are also angelic measurements." Does this passage mean that this wall is 72 yards thick, or 72 yards high, or both? If you read certain Old Testament descriptions of walls, sometimes the height is given, sometimes the thickness is given.

If we go with the view that the city is a large skyscraper cube, then the 72 yards most likely does not refer to the wall's height, for a city that is 1500 miles in height is not contained by a wall that is 72 yards in height. So as the golden cube exists, it would be 72 yards thick. In ancient times, the emphasis of a wall was on its height. So the 72-yard height would fit better if you were to take the view that the New Jerusalem is more like a land mass, and not so much an encased cube.

The New Jerusalem is made of precious materials ranging from stones to precious metals, all of various colors. Revelation 21:22 says there is no temple in the city because God and the Lamb are its temple. God and the Lamb's presence are so manifested in this city there is no need for a temple.

Verse 23 continues, "The city has no need of the sun or of the moon to shine on it, for the glory of God has illumined it, and its lamp is the Lamb." The New Jerusalem is so illumined by God that it does not need any other light source. This is not necessarily a statement that the sun or moon do not exist, but they are not needed to light the New Jerusalem.

Verse 24 says, "The nations will walk by its light, and the kings of the earth will bring their glory into it." This refers to literal geopolitical nations. Kings exist, which most likely means that governmental functions are taking place. And because we are on the new earth, these nations and kings are followers of the King. While nations are a post-Fall development (Genesis 10–11), their mention here indicates that God desires the presence of multiple nations on the new earth.

These rulers "will bring the glory and the honor of the nations into it" (verse 26). It seems these nations will use all their talents and gifts and some would even say cultural contributions for the glory of God, and they will make their contributions in the New Jerusalem.

The Tree of Life

A ninth detail is the prominence of the tree of life. In Revelation 22:1-2 we read, "Then he showed me a river of the water of life, clear as crystal, coming from the throne of God and of the Lamb…on either side of the river was the tree of life." The last time anyone witnessed the tree of life was back in the garden in Genesis 3. After the fall, Adam and Eve were barred from eating from the tree of life. God sent an angel to guard the tree so that Adam and Eve would not have access to it. But in the New Jerusalem on the new earth, we will see the tree of life, and it will bear 12 kinds of fruit. It will yield its fruit every month, which seems to indicate that time will exist in the eternal state.

The leaves of the tree have a unique function—they will be used for "the healing of the nations" (verse 2). This does not mean nations will be at war with one another; instead, the leaves of the tree will maintain perpetual harmony among the nations. The nations once at war will be in harmony. Access to this tree will no longer be barred. It will be accessible to all on the new earth.

Eternal Fellowship

The tenth and final observation concerns our fellowship with and service of God. "There will no longer be any curse; and the throne of God and of the Lamb will be in it, and His bond-servants will serve Him" (Revelation 22:3). We learn in verse 4 that we will see God's face and His name will be on our foreheads—an indication of intimate fellowship. "There will no longer be any night; and they will not have need of the light of a lamp nor the light of the sun, because the Lord God will illumine them" (verse 5). The new earth will enjoy the presence and light of God for all of eternity: "They will reign forever and ever" (verse 5).

The coming eternal state should thrill our hearts. Everything we do now and everything we are fighting for is pointing toward this period in history. No matter what we go through now, no matter what sorrow, tears, or tragedies we face, when we are on that new earth, it will all have been worth it. We are going to be so focused on God and what He has prepared for us that everything negative that ever happened in this life is going to be forgotten. We will fellowship with our God and Savior and all those who love Him.

NOTES

Chapter 1—The Lord's Greatest Prayer, Part 1

1. Sinclair Ferguson, *The Christian Life* (Edinburgh: Banner of Truth, 2013), 6.

Chapter 3—Adam, Where Art Thou?

1. Peter Enns, *The Evolution of Adam: What the Bible Does and Doesn't Say about Human Origins* (Grand Rapids: Brazos Press, 2012), 66.

2. Jeffrey Burton Russell, *Inventing the Flat Earth* (Westport, CT: Praeger, 1997), 76.

3. Noel Weeks, "Cosmology in Historical Context," *Westminster Theological Journal* 68, no. 2 (2006): 283-93.

4. Jonathan F. Henry, "Uniformitarianism in Old Testament Studies: A Review of *Ancient Near Eastern Thought and the Old Testament* by John H. Walton," *Journal of Dispensational Theology* 13, no. 39 (2009): 19-36 (esp. 25-28).

5. Paul Joüon, *A Grammar of Biblical Hebrew*, trans. and rev. T. Muraoka, *Subsidia Biblica* 14/I–II (Rome: Pontifical Biblical Institute, 1993), 2:376 (§114*e* n. 1).

Chapter 4—Why Every Self-Respecting Calvinist Must Be a Six-Day Creationist

1. Jonathan Edwards, *Miscellany* no. 547, 1731.

2. Blaine Harden, "The Greening of Evangelicals: Christian Right Turns, Sometimes Warily, to Environmentalism," *Washington Post* (February 6, 2005), A01.

3. Declaration of the Care of Creation, Evangelical Environmental Network and *Creation Care* magazine, 1994, http://www.creationcare.org/evangelical_declaration_of_the_care_of_creation.

4. Declaration of the Care of Creation.

5. Declaration of the Care of Creation.

Chapter 5—Faith of Our Fathers

1. Cf. Philip Schaff, *A History of the Christian Church* (New York: Charles Scribner's Sons, 1916), 6:128.

2. Schaff, 129-30.

3. Schaff, 130.

4. Martin Luther. Trans. from James M. Kittelson, *Luther the Reformer: The Story of the Man and His Career* (Minneapolis: Fortress Press, 2003), 134.

5. Francis Beckwith originally published these comments on his blog in May 2007. Cf. Todd Pruit, "Beckwith Back to Rome," *The Alliance of Confessing Evangelicals* (July 30, 2007), http://www.alliancenet.org/mos/1517/beckwith-back-to-rome.

6. In verses 20-21, James asked Gentile Christians to stay away from idolatry and immorality, and to be sensitive to the weaker consciences of their Jewish brothers and sisters, which fits perfectly with Paul's instruction about weaker brothers in Romans 14–15 and 1 Corinthians 8–9.

7. Cf. Thomas Oden, *The Justification Reader* (Grand Rapids: Eerdmans, 2002). Also see Nick Needham, "Justification in the Early Church Fathers," in *Justification in Perspective*, ed. Bruce L. McCormack, 25–53 (Grand Rapids: Baker Academic, 2006), 40.

8. Clement of Rome, *1 Clem.* 32.4. Trans. from Michael W. Holmes, ed. *The Apostolic Fathers* (Grand Rapids: Baker Academic, 2007), 87.

9. Polycarp, *Pol. Phil.* 1.2-3. Trans. from Holmes, *The Apostolic Fathers*, 281.

10. *Diogn.* 9.2-5. Trans. from Oden, *The Justification Reader*, 65.

11. Cf. Martin Luther, *A Commentary on St. Paul's Epistle to the Galatians*, trans. Erasmus Middleton, ed. John Prince Fallowes (Grand Rapids: Kregel, 1979), 172.

12. Hilary, *Comm. Matt.* 20.7. *PL* 9.1030. Trans. from Hilary of Poitiers, *Commentary on Matthew*, The Fathers of the Church, trans. D.H. Williams (Washington, DC: The Catholic University of America Press, 2012), 212.

13. Hilary, 8.6. *PL* 9.961. Trans. from D.H. Williams, "Justification by Faith: A Patristic Doctrine," 658.

14. Basil, *Hom. humil.* 20.3. *PG* 31.529. Trans. from Elowsky, *We Believe in the Holy Spirit*, 98.

15. Ambrosiaster, *Ad Rom.*, on Rom. 3:24. *PL* 17.79. Trans. from Elowsky, *We Believe in the Holy Spirit*, 98.

16. Ambrosiaster, on Rom. 3:27. *PL* 17.80. Trans. from Bray, *Romans*, ACCS, 103.

17. Ambrosiaster, on Rom. 4:6. *PL* 17.83. Trans. from Bray, *Romans*, ACCS, 113.

18. John Chrysostom, *Hom. Rom.* 7 (on Rom. 3:27). *PG* 60.446. Trans. from *NPNF*, First Series, 11.379.

19. John Chrysostom, *Hom. 1 Cor.* 8 (on 1 Cor. 3:1-3). *PG* 61.73. Trans. from *NPNF*, First Series, 12.47.

20. John Chrysostom, *Hom. Gal.*, on Gal. 3:8. *PG* 61.651. Trans. from *NPNF*, First Series, 13.26.

21. John Chrysostom, on Gal. 3:12. *PG* 61.652. Trans. from *NPNF*, First Series, 13:26.

22. John Chrysostom, *Hom. 1 Tim.*, on 1 Tim. 1:15-16. *PG* 62.520-21. Trans. from Elowsky, *We Believe in the Holy Spirit*, 98.

23. John Chrysostom, *Adv. Jud.* 7.3. *PG* 48.919.

24. Marius Victorinus, *Ep. Eph.* 1 (on Eph. 2:7). *PL* 8.1255. Cf. Oden, *The Justification Reader*, 48.

25. Victorinus, 1 (on Eph. 2.9). *PL* 8.1256. Trans. from Oden, *The Justification Reader*, 48. Cf. Marius Victorinus, *Epistle to the Galatians* 2.3.21.

26. Victorinus, 1 (on Eph. 2:15). *PL* 8.1258. Trans. from Joseph A. Fitzmyer, *Romans: A New Translation with Introduction and Commentary by Joseph A. Fitzmyer*, The Anchor Bible, vol. 33 (New York: Doubleday, 1993), 361.

27. Marius Victorinus, *Epistle to the Galatians*, 1.3.7. Trans. From Mark J. Edwards, ed., Galatians, Ephesians, Philippians, ACCS, 39.

28. Augustine, *Enarrat. Ps.*, 31.7. *PL* 36.263. Trans. from John E. Rotelle, *Expositions of the Psalms 1–32* (Hyde Park: New City Press, 2000), 11.370.

29. Augustine, *Tractates on the Gospel of John*, John 1:15-18, Tractate 3.9 in *NPNF*, 7:21; cited from Gregg R. Allison, *Historical Theology*, 501.

30. Augustine, *Spir. et litt.* 13 (22). *PL* 44.214-15. Trans. from *NPNF*, First Series, 5:93.

31. Prosper of Aquitaine, *Voc. Gent.*, 1.17. *PL* 51.669. Trans. from Oden, *The Justification Reader*, 46.

32. Theodoret, *Interp. Rom.*, on Rom. 4:4. *PG* 82.88. Trans. from Bray, *Romans*, ACCS, 108.

33. Theodoret, on Rom. 1:17. *PG* 82.57, 60. Trans. from Bray, *Romans*, ACCS, 31.

34. Theodoret, *Interp. Eph.*, on Eph. 2:4-5. *PG* 82.520. Trans. from Oden, *The Justification Reader*, 113.

35. Theodoret, on Eph. 2:8-9. *PG* 82.521. Trans. from Oden, *The Justification Reader*, 44.

36. Theodoret, *Epist.* 83. *PG* 83.1269. Trans. from Elowsky, *We Believe in the Holy Spirit*, 99.

37. Both citations from Anselm of Canterbury, *Admon. mor. PL* 158:686-687. Trans. from *Meditations and Prayers*, 275-77.

38. Bernard of Clairvaux, *Epist.* 190.6. *PL* 182.1065. Trans. from John Mabillon, ed., *Life and Works of Saint Bernard, Abbot of Clairvaux*, trans. Samuel J. Eales (London: John Hodges, 1889), 2.580-581.

39. St. Bernard as recorded by William of St. Thierry, *S. Bern. vit. prim.* 1.12. *PL* 185.258. Trans. from Alban Butler, *The Lives of the Fathers, Martyrs, and Other Principal Saints*, vol. 8 (Dublin: James Duffy, 1845), 231.

40. Bernard of Clairvaux, *Serm. Cant.* 22.8. *PL* 183.881. Trans. from Franz Posset, *Pater Bernhardus*, 186.

41. Norman Geisler and Josh Betancourt, *Is Rome the True Church?* (Wheaton, IL: Crossway, 2008), 53-54.

42. Gregg R. Allison, *Historical Theology* (Grand Rapids: Zondervan, 2011), 505.

43. John Calvin, "Dedicatory Letter to Francis I," *Institutes*, section 4.

Chapter 7—The Extent of the Atonement

1. Robert Charles Hill, trans., *Theodoret of Cyrus: Commentary on the Letters of St. Paul*, vol. 2 (Brookline: Holy Cross Orthodox Press, 2001), 175.

2. Teodosia Tomkinson, trans., *Ambrose: Exposition of the Holy Gospel According to St. Luke* (Etna, CA: Center for Traditionalist Orthodox Studies, 1998), 201-202.

3. Cited in George Musgrave Giger, trans., *Francis Turretin: Institutes of Elenctic Theology*, 3 vols. (Phillipsburg, NJ: P&R, 1994), 2:462.

4. John Owen, trans., *Commentaries on the Catholic Epistles by John Calvin* (Grand Rapids: Eerdmans, 1948), 173.

5. Thomas J. Nettles, *By His Grace and for His Glory* (Lake Charles, LA: Cor Meum Tibi, 2002), 320.

6. R.B. Kuiper, *For Whom Did Christ Die?* (Grand Rapids: Eerdmans, 1959), 78 (emphasis added).

7. Charles Haddon Spurgeon, *The Metropolitan Tabernacle Pulpit*, 63 vols. (London: Passmore & Alabaster, 1903), 49:39.

8. Robert Smith Candlish, *The Atonement: Its Efficacy and Extent* (Edinburgh: Adam and Charles Black, 1867), 173.

9. Archibald Alexander Hodge, *The Atonement* (Philadelphia: Presbyterian Board of Publication, 1867), 359.

10. Kuiper, *For Whom Did Christ Die?*, 83-84.

11. Kuiper, *For Whom Did Christ Die?*, 84 (emphasis added).

12. Kuiper, *For Whom Did Christ Die?*, 85.

13. Kuiper, *For Whom Did Christ Die?*

14. Thomas Myers, trans., *Calvin: Commentary on the First Twenty Chapters of the Book of the Prophet Ezekiel* (Grand Rapids: Eerdmans, 1948), 246-247.

15. Charles Hodge, *Systematic Theology*, 3 vols. (New York: Scribners, 1872), 2:546.

16. Curt Daniel, *The History and Theology of Calvinism* (Dallas: Scholarly Reprints, 1993), 368.

Chapter 8—A Biblical Case for Elder Rule

1. George Barna, *Revolution* (Wheaton, IL: Tyndale, 2005), 37.

2. Donald Miller, *The Nature and Mission of the Church*, quoted in Robert Saucy, *The Church in God's Program* (Chicago: Moody Press, 1972), 105.

3. Miller, quoted in Saucy, 105.

4. Alexander Strauch, *Biblical Eldership* (Littleton, CO: Lewis & Roth Publishers, 1995), 101.

5. J.B. Lightfoot, "The Christian Ministry" in *St. Paul's Epistle to the Philippians* (London: MacMillan & Co., 1898), 186.

6. Robert Saucy, *The Church in God's Program* (Chicago: Moody Press, 1972), 112.

7. Saucy, *The Church in God's Program*, 112.

8. Wayne Grudem, *Systematic Theology* (Grand Rapids, MI: Zondervan, 1994), 926.

9. Polycarp, *Philippians*, 5, 6.

Chapter 9—The Great Commission as a Theological Endeavor

1. Robert Jamieson, A. R. Fausset, and David Brown, *Commentary Critical and Explanatory on the Whole Bible*, vol. 2 (Oak Harbor, WA: Logos Research Systems, Inc., 1997), 64.

2. The magazine I refer to is *Heart Cry*. For more on this publication, see http://www.heartcrymissionary.com/heartcry-magazine-archive.

3. Craig Blomberg, *Matthew*, vol. 22, The New American Commentary (Nashville: Broadman & Holman Publishers, 1992), 431.

4. William Carey, as cited in Peter Morden, *Offering Christ to the World: Andrew Fuller (1754–1815) and the Revival of Eighteenth Century Particular Baptist Life*, Studies in Baptist History and Thought 8 (Carlisle: Paternoster, 2003), 136.

Chapter 10—Why Every Self-Respecting Calvinist Must Be a Premillennialist

1. Oswald T. Allis, *Prophecy and the Church* (Philadelphia: P&R Publishing, [1945] 1947), 238.

2. Floyd E. Hamilton, *The Basis of Millennial Faith* (Grand Rapids, MI: Eerdmans, 1955), 38-39.

3. Herman Bavinck, *Reformed Dogmatics: Abridged in One Volume* (Grand Rapids, MI: Baker, 2011), 658.

4. William Cuninghame, *The Pre-Millennial Advent of Messiah Demonstrated from the Scriptures* (London: Nisbet, 1836).

5. Manuel Lacunza y Diaz, *The Coming of Messiah in Glory and Majesty* (London: L.B. Seeley and Sons, 1827).

6. Emil Schurer, *A History of the Jewish People in the Time of Jesus,* 5 volumes (Peabody, MA: Hendrickson, 1993).

7. Ronald Diprose, *Israel and the Church* (Downers Grove, IL: InterVarsity Press, 2004).

Chapter 11—Heaven on Earth

1. Randy Alcorn's book *Heaven* is one notable exception.

2. A.F. Johnson, "Revelation," in F.E. Gaebelein, ed., *The Expositor's Bible Commentary, Volume 12: Hebrews Through Revelation* (Grand Rapids, MI: Zondervan, 1981), 592.

John MacArthur is pastor-teacher of Grace Community Church in Sun Valley, California, and president of The Master's University and Seminary.

William Barrick is faculty associate and director of ThD studies at The Master's Seminary. He is also the Old Testament editor for the Evangelical Exegetical Commentary.

Nathan Busenitz is an assistant professor of theology at The Master's Seminary and an elder at Grace Community Church in Sun Valley, California.

R.C. Sproul is the founder and chairman of Ligonier Ministries and senior minister of preaching and teaching at Saint Andrew's in Sanford, Florida.

Phil Johnson is the executive director of Grace to You and primary editor of John MacArthur's books. He is also an elder at Grace Community Church in Sun Valley, California.

Tom Pennington is the pastor-teacher of Countryside Bible Church in Southlake, Texas.

Paul Washer is the founder of HeartCry Missionary Society, which supports indigenous missionaries throughout Africa, Asia, Europe, the Middle East, and Latin America.

Michael J. Vlach is a professor of theology at The Master's Seminary and specializes in the areas of systematic theology, historical theology, apologetics, and world religions.

GET THE COMPLETE
SHEPHERDS' LIBRARY SERIES

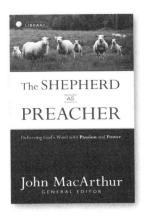

The Shepherd as Preacher
John MacArthur, General Editor

Scripture holds a simple declaration that sets forth every pastor's highest priority: "Preach the Word."

Such an enormous responsibility deserves every pastor's best. In *The Shepherd as Preacher*—a compilation of powerful messages from the annual Shepherds' Conference at Grace Community Church—you'll survey the essentials every minister needs to know, including...

- the focus and purpose of biblical preaching
- the character of a faithful preacher
- the keys to effective preaching
- how to preach in the Spirit's power

Yours is a high and holy privilege—one with incredible potential to change lives. This book will equip you to fulfill that calling with excellence.

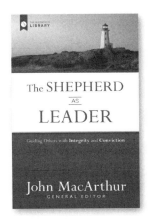

The Shepherd as Leader
John MacArthur, General Editor

How are you doing when it comes to being the kind of leader your church needs?

The *Shepherd as Leader* brings together the most memorable messages on leadership from the internationally recognized Shepherds' Conference held at Grace Community Church, pastored by John MacArthur. Contributors such as John Piper, Albert Mohler Jr., Steven J. Lawson, and others offer timeless guidance on...

- the characteristics of a faithful leader
- the urgency of purity and integrity in a leader's life
- the necessity and practice of prayer
- a proper response to opposition and suffering
- the leader's need for a heart of true humility

Every leadership principle in this book was modeled by Christ Himself—the best leader we could ever learn from.

To learn more about Harvest House books and
to read sample chapters, visit our website:

www.harvesthousepublishers.com

HARVEST HOUSE PUBLISHERS
EUGENE, OREGON